P.S. I color

Birds 1

An Adult Coloring Book Series

Relaxation. Therapeutic. Fun!!!

© 2015

For Jaymin, Laura, Lola Eve & Silvie-Lace

Love to color

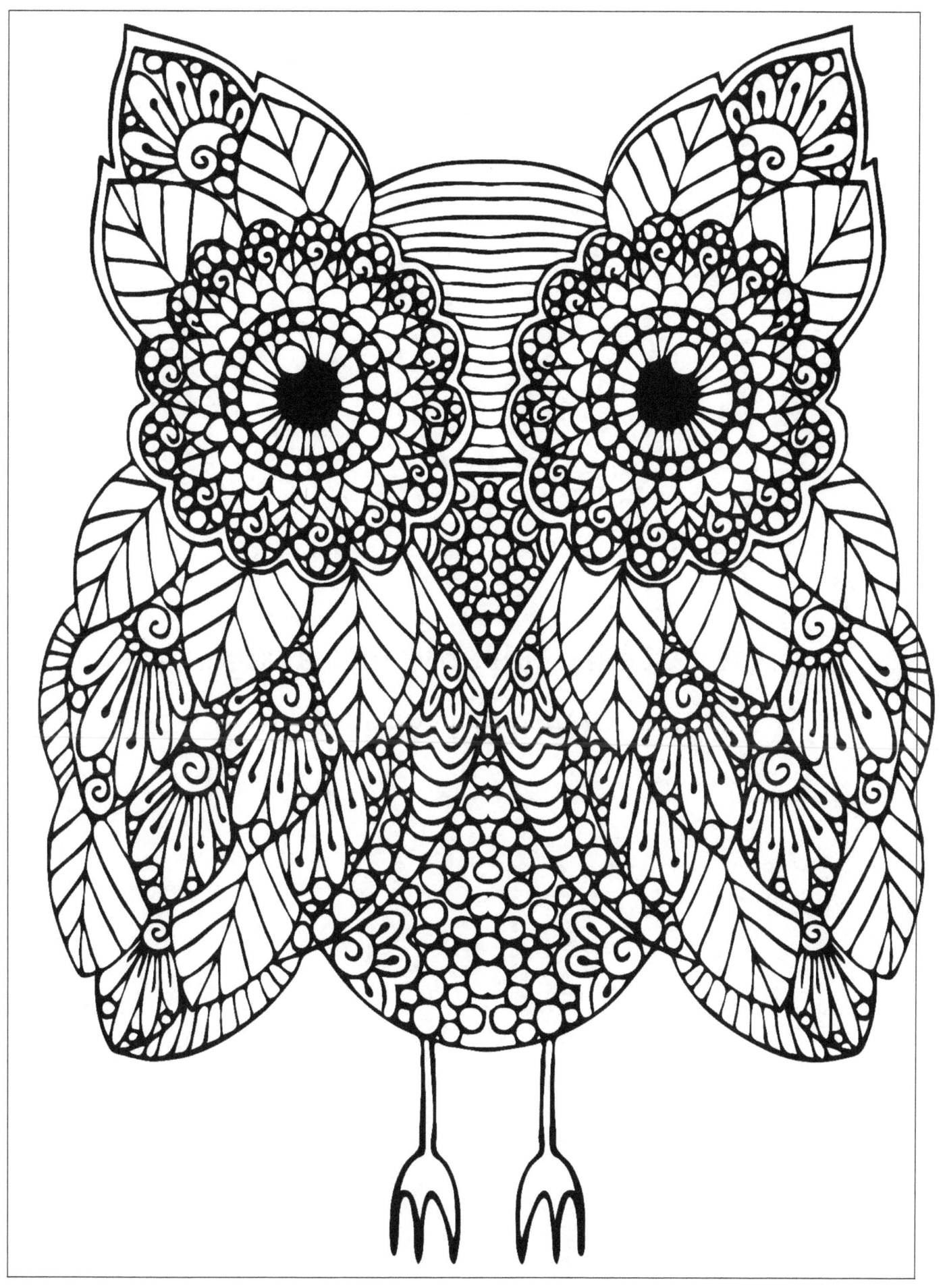

Level 3

A forest bird never wants a cage.

- Henrik Ibsen

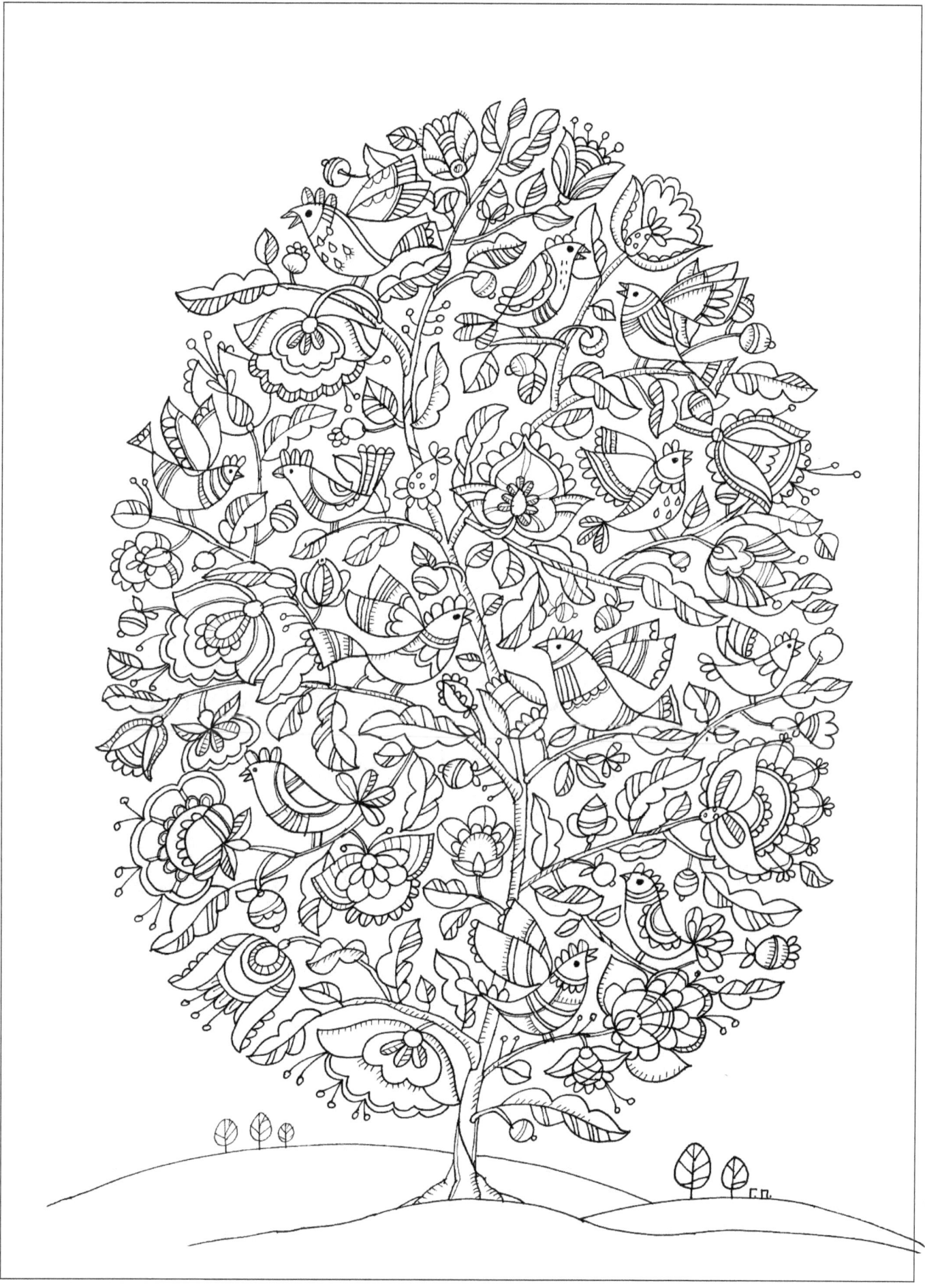

Level 2

The early bird catches the first worm.

- Author Unknown.

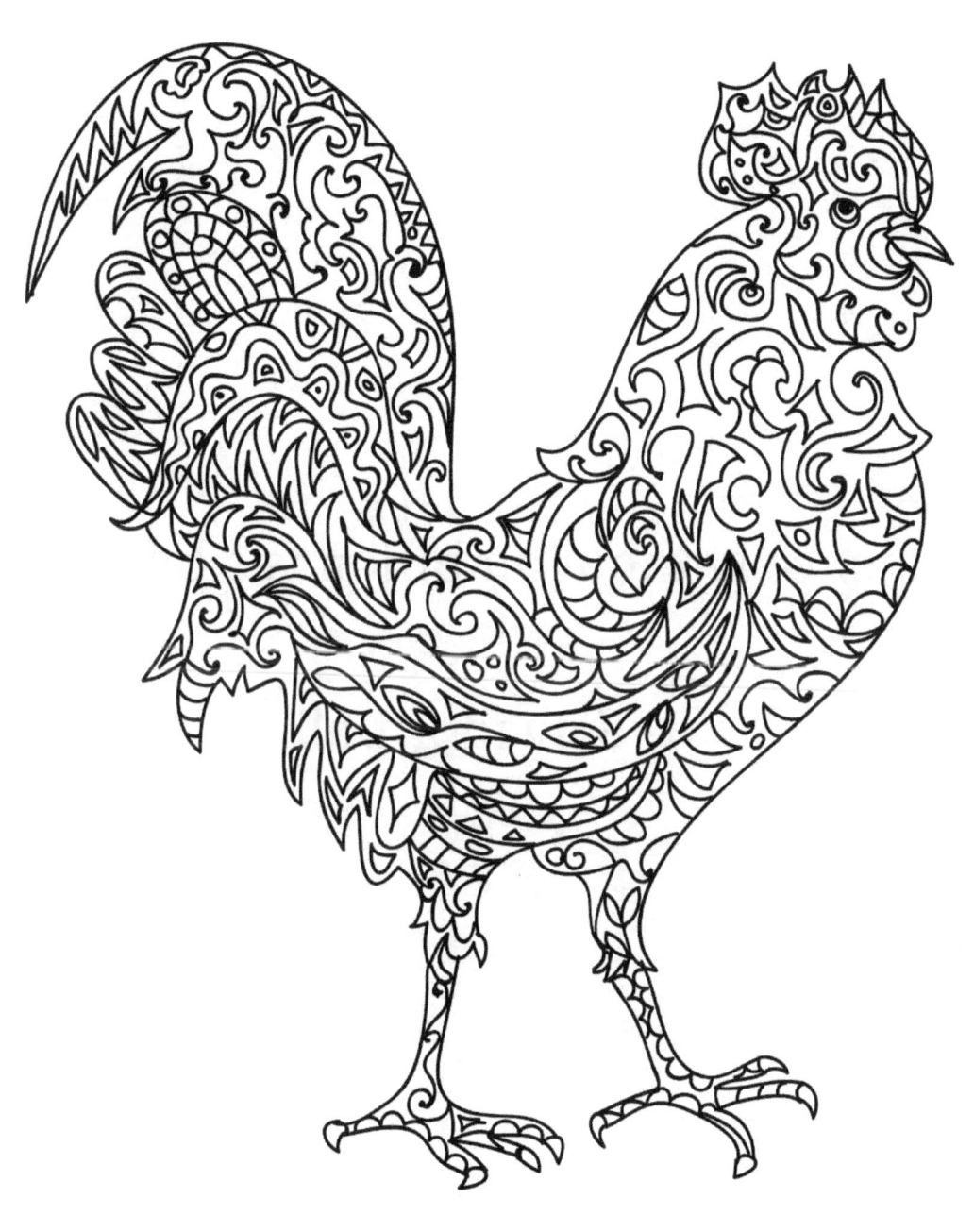

Level 1

Intelligence without ambition is a bird without wings.

- Salvador Dali

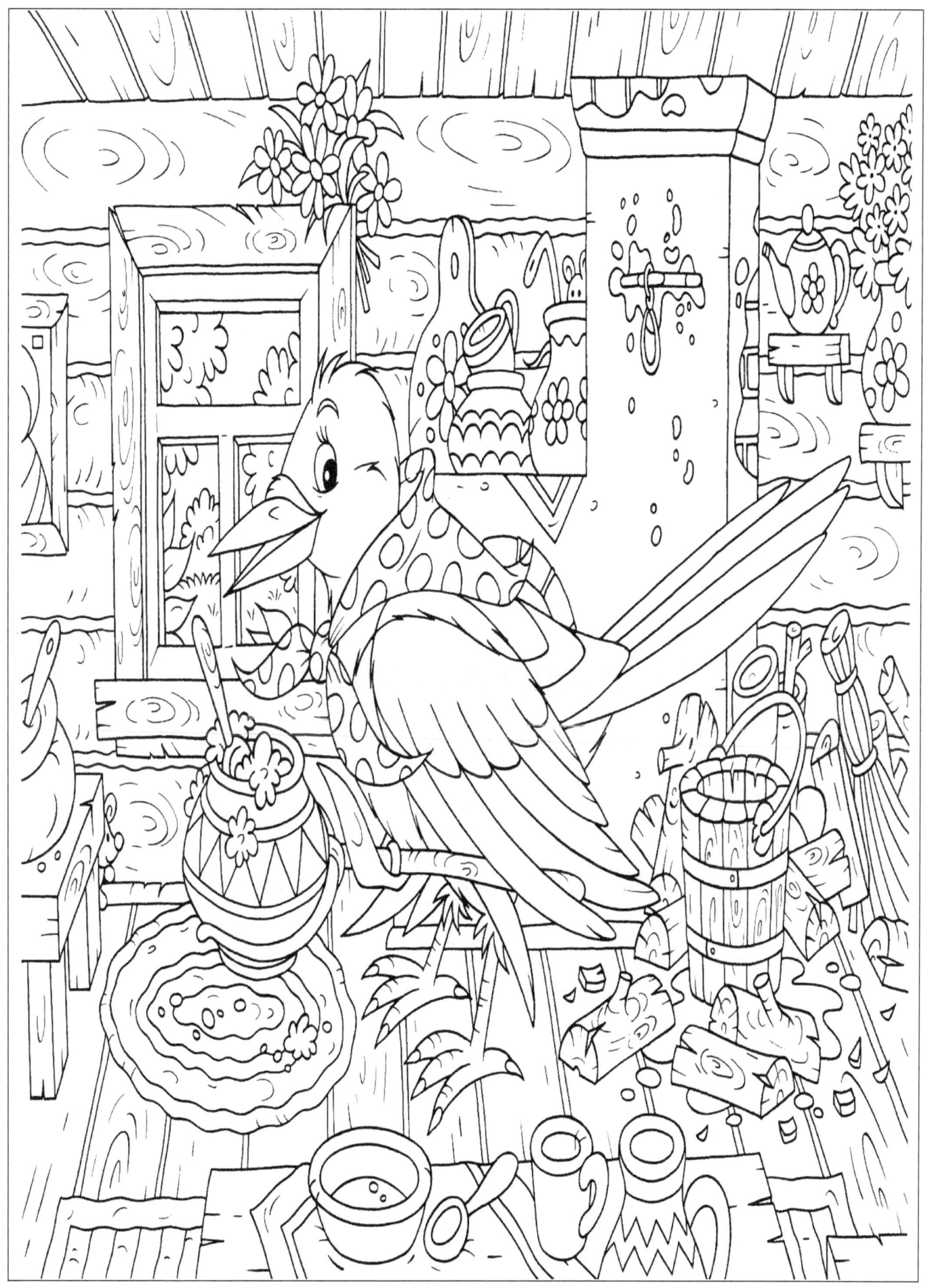

Level 1

Being human is exhausting,

so be an owl

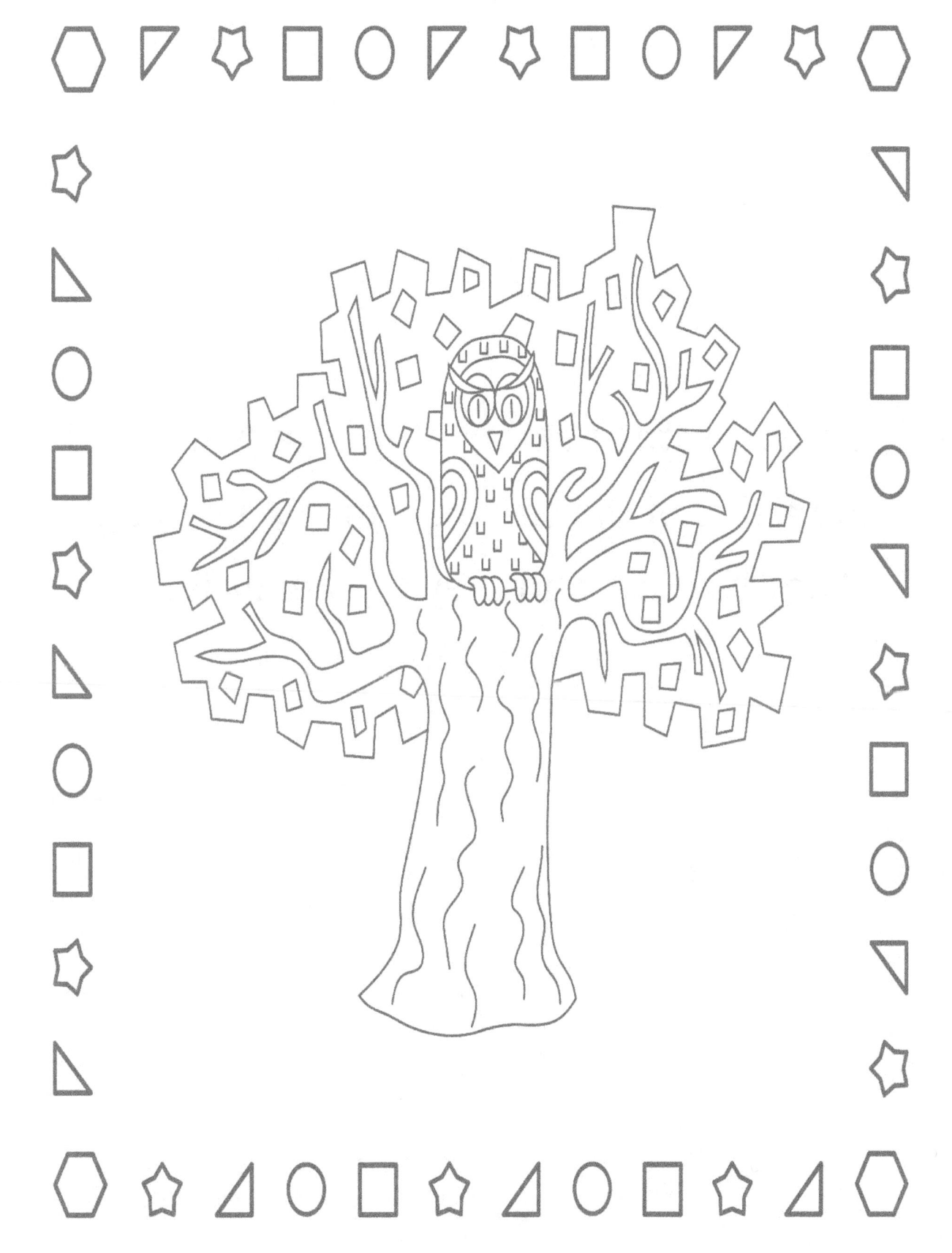

Level 2

I don't ask for the meaing of the song of a bird

or the rising of the sun on a misty morning.

They just are, and they are beautiful.

- Pete Hamill

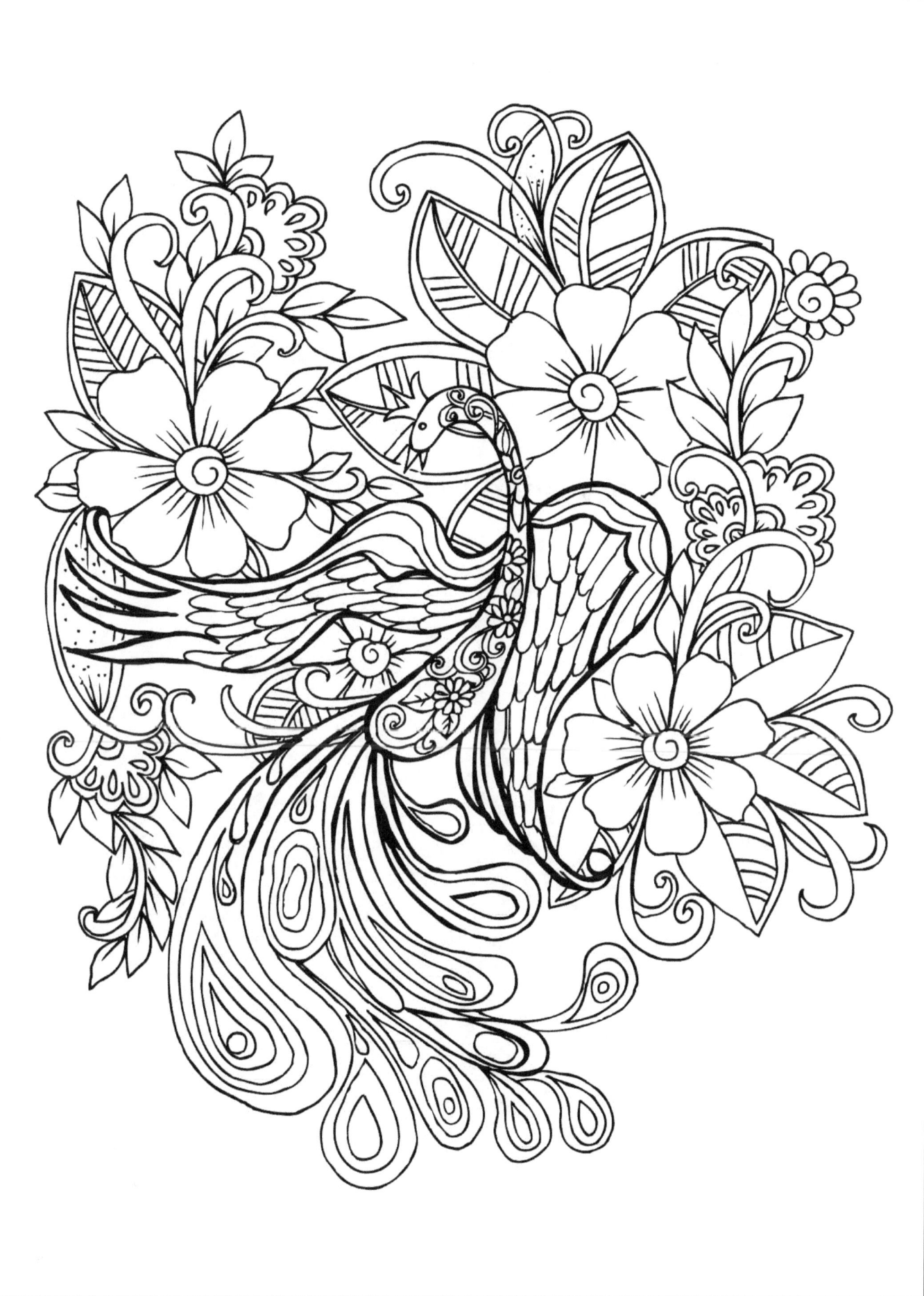

Level 3

Grow wise little owl.

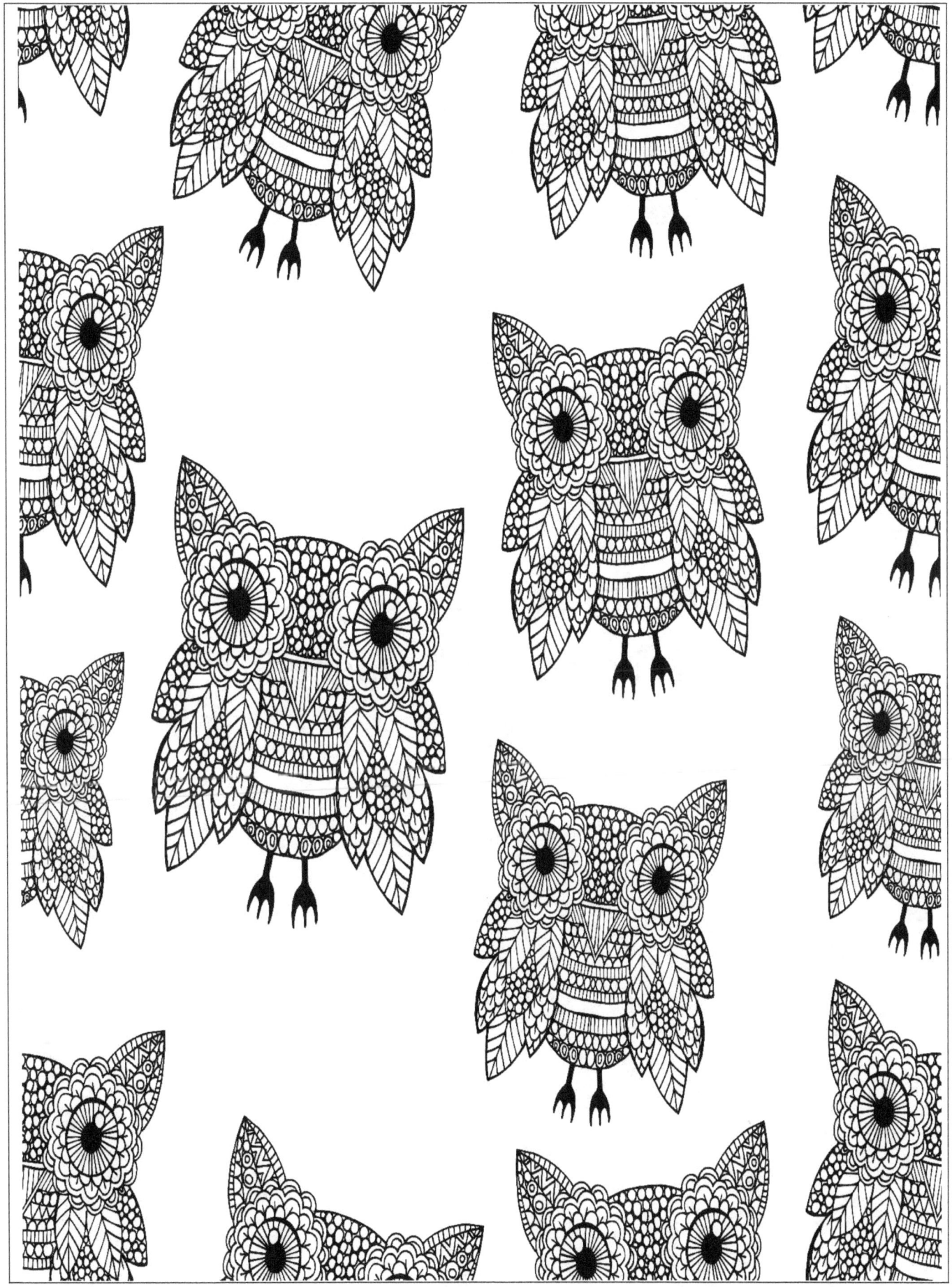

Level 1

Don't cry because it's over,
smile because it happened.
- Dr Seuss

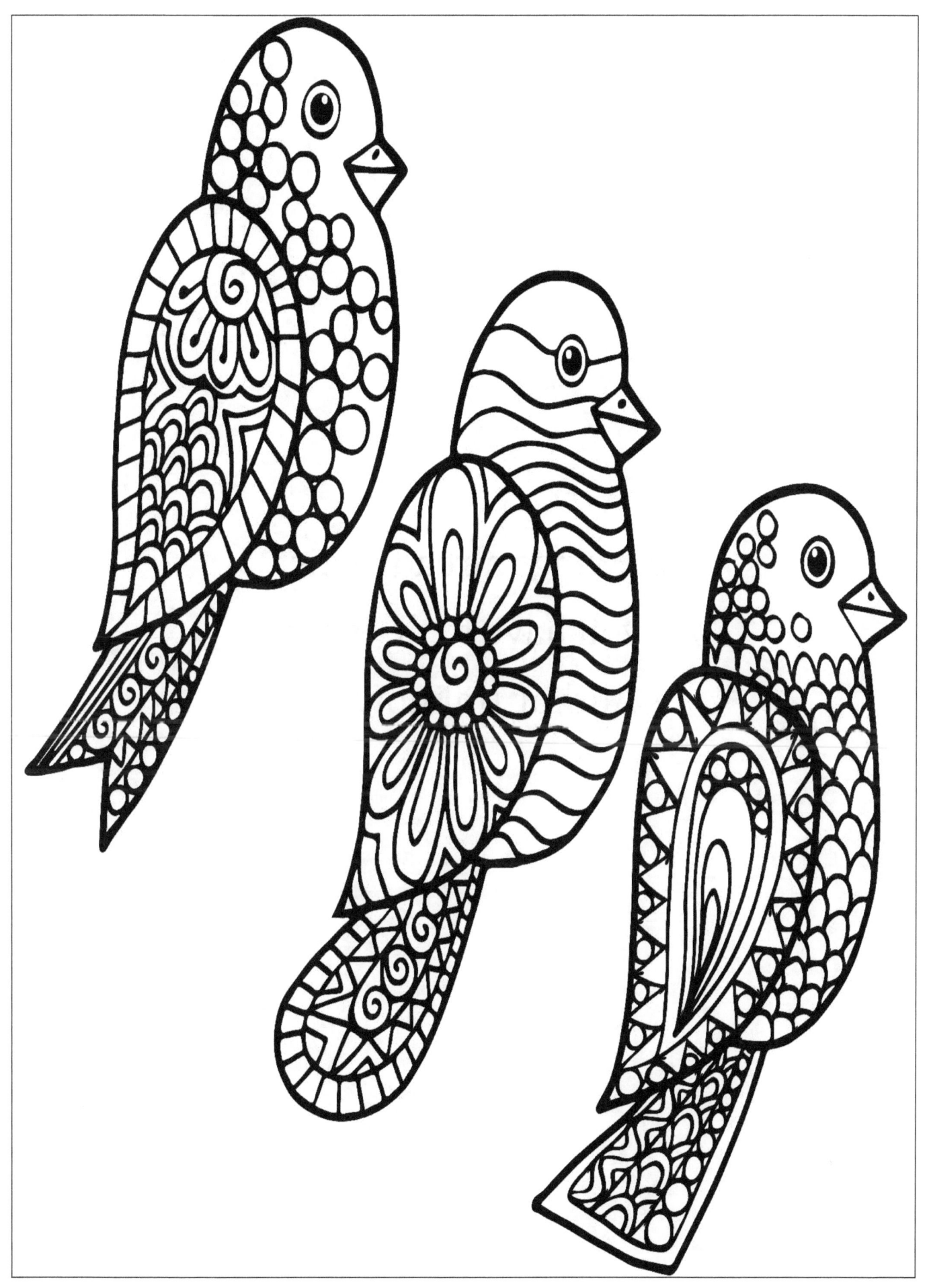

Level 2

Your wings already exist.

All you have to do is fly.

- Author Unknown.

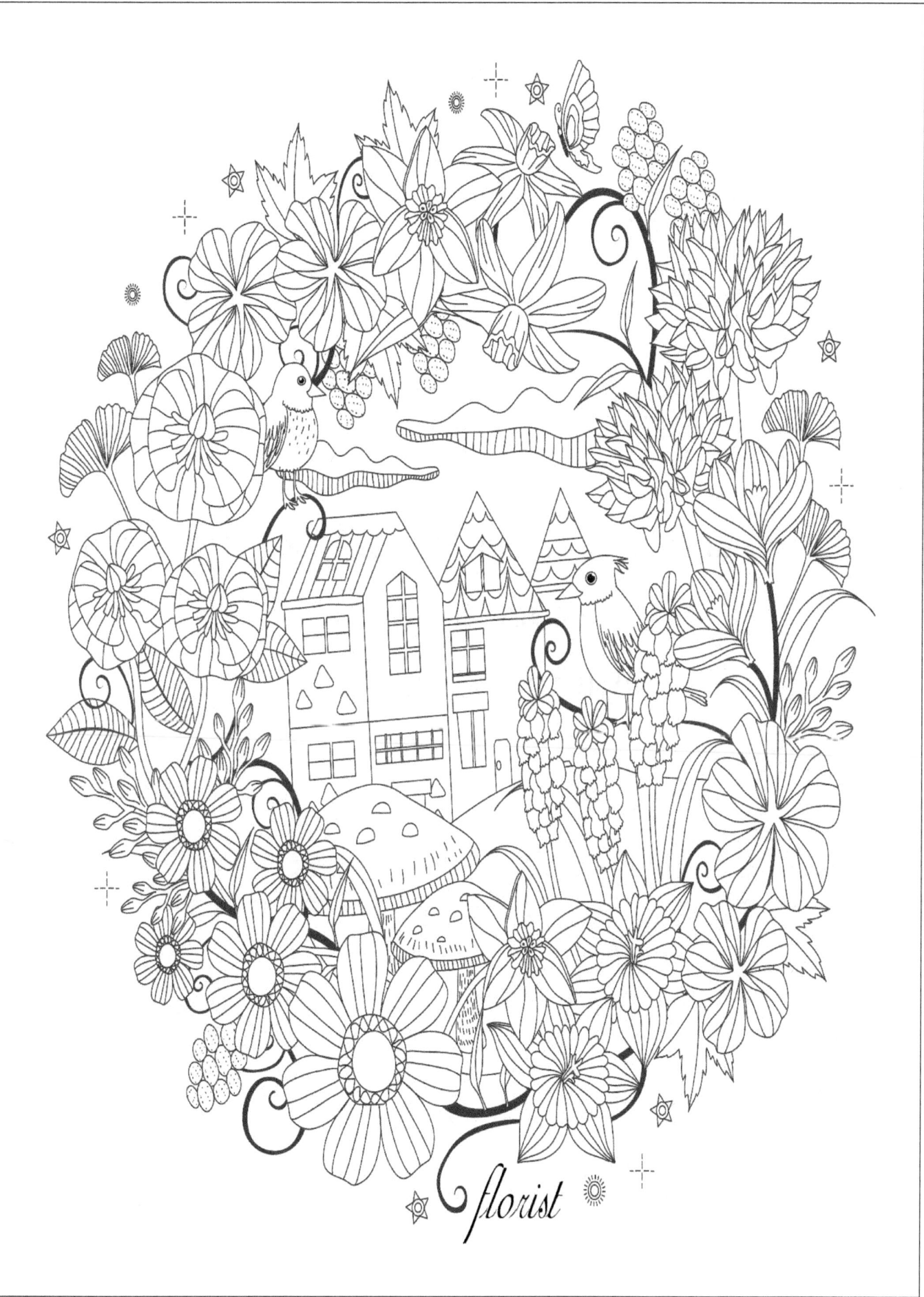

florist

Level 2

Observe and reflect and become a little wiser each day.

-Author Unknown

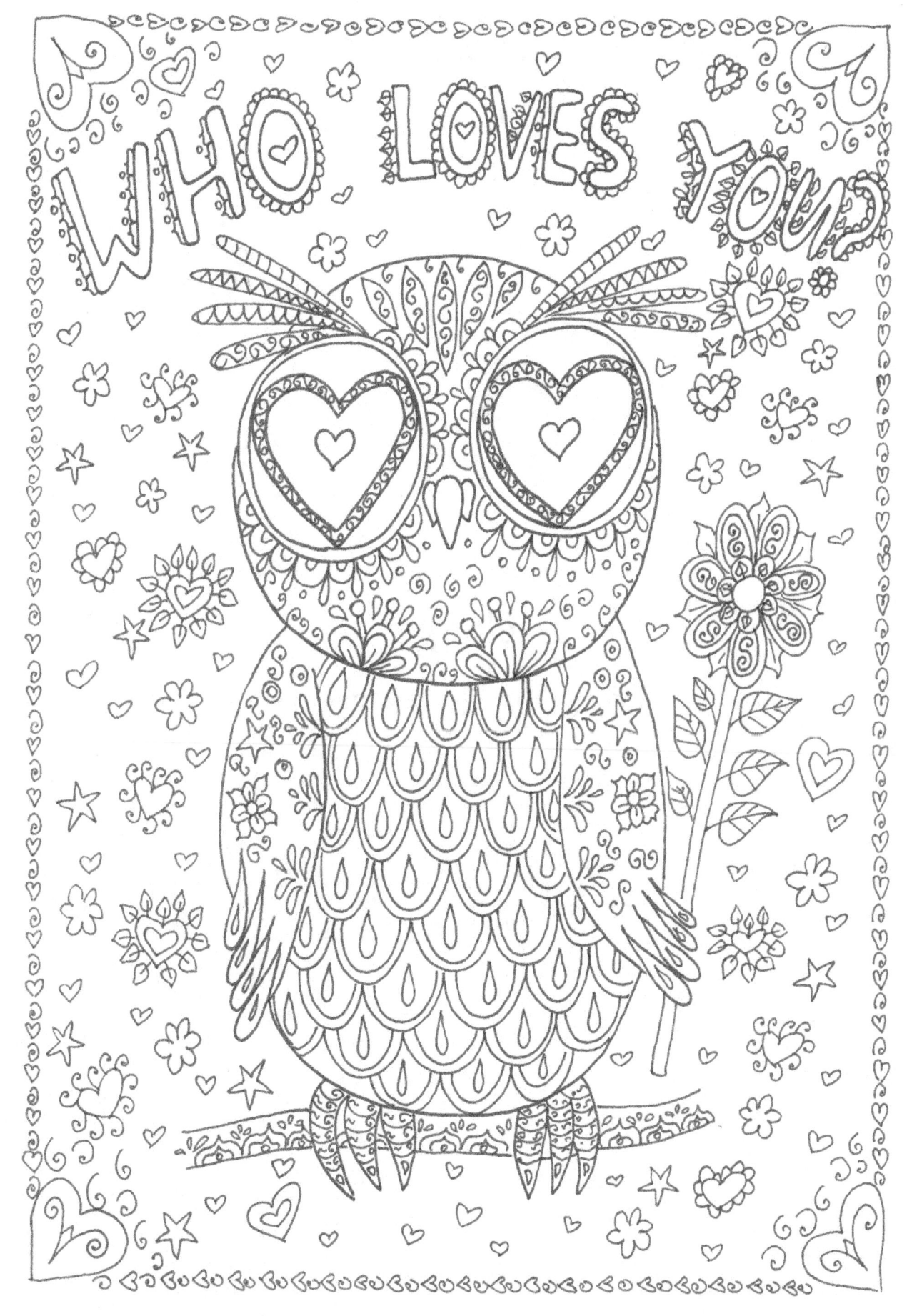

Level 2

Pack up.

Let's fly, fly away.

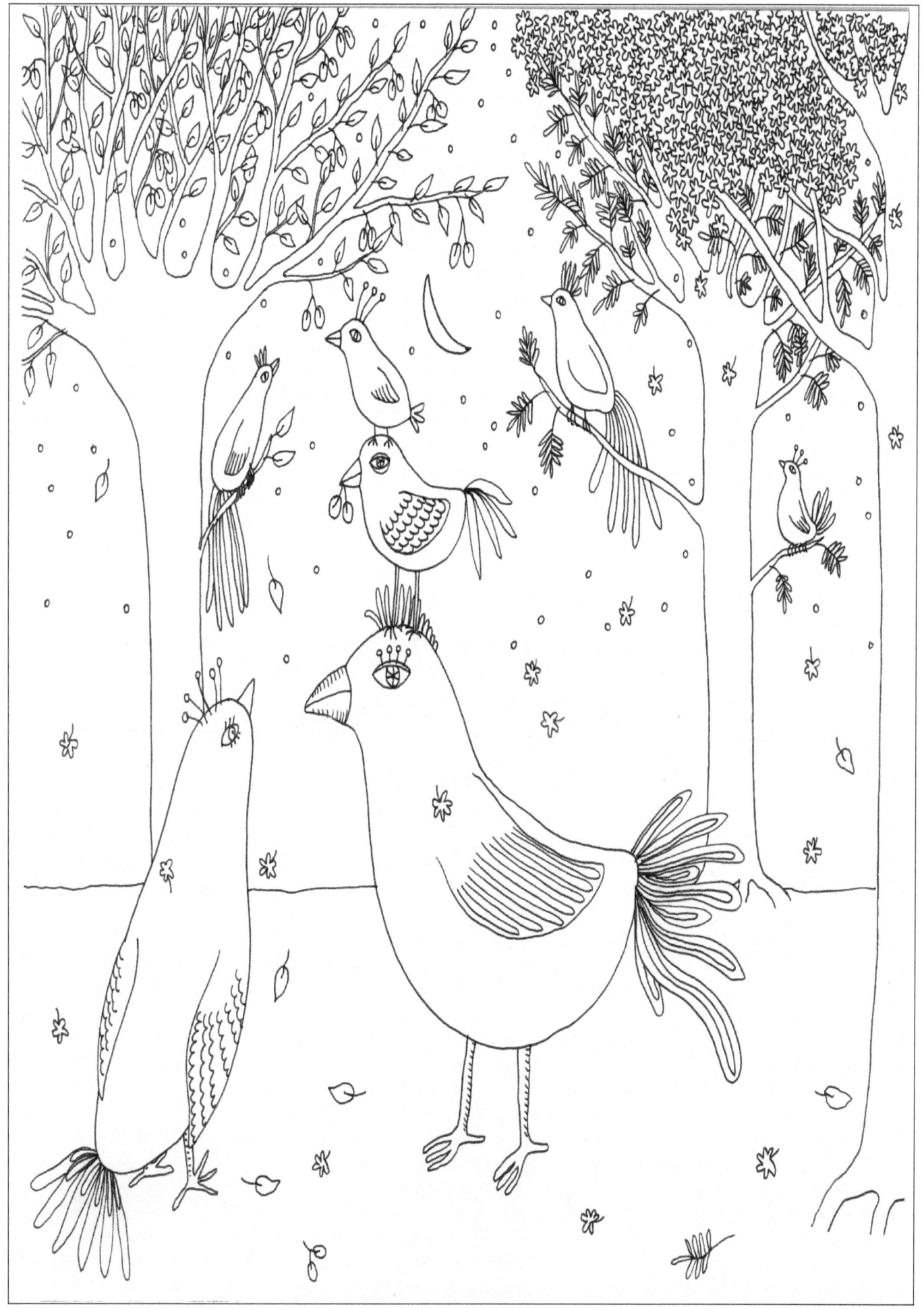

Level 2

Don't be scared to fly alone.

Find a path that is your own.

- Author Unknown.

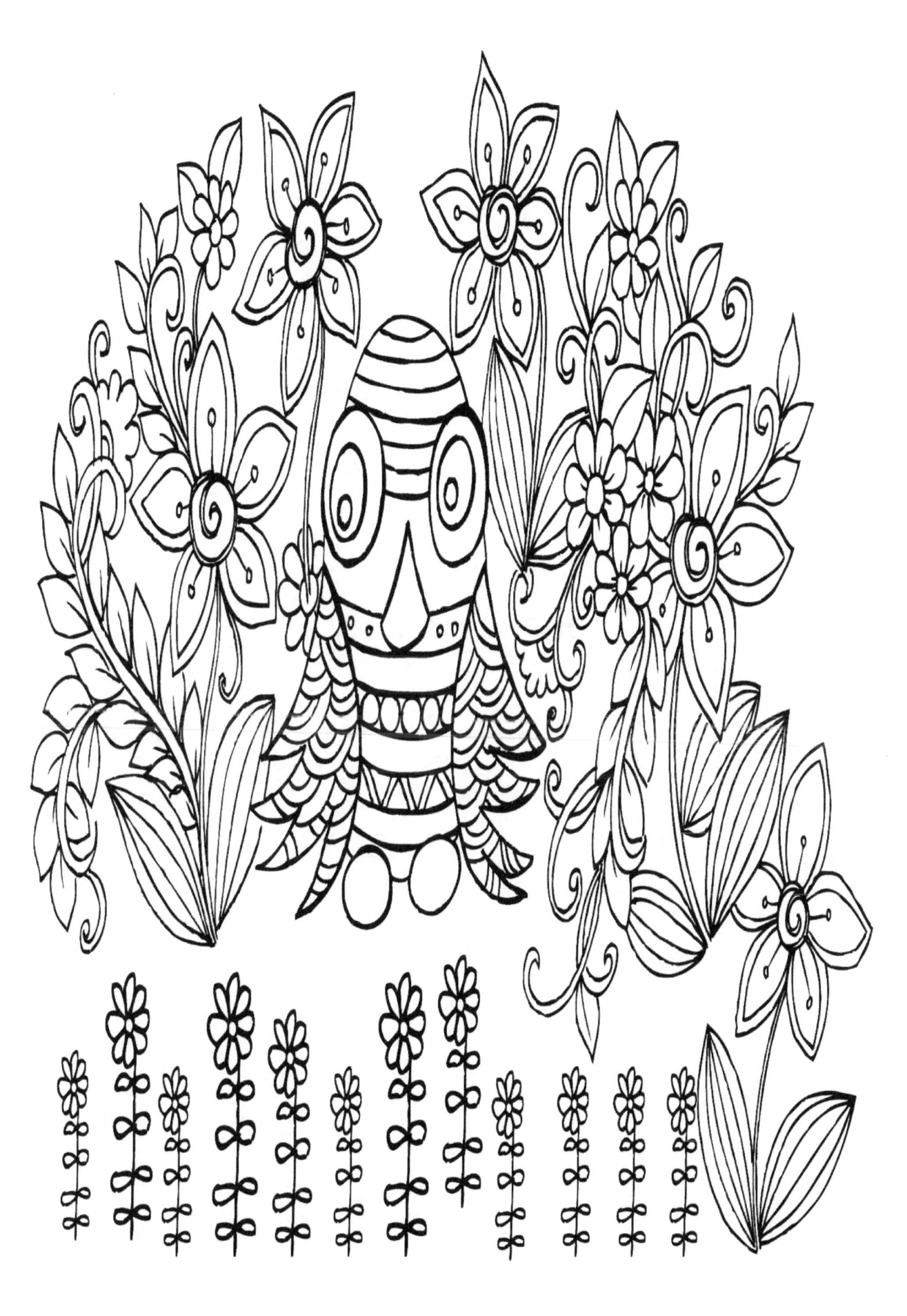

Level 3

I believe I can fly.

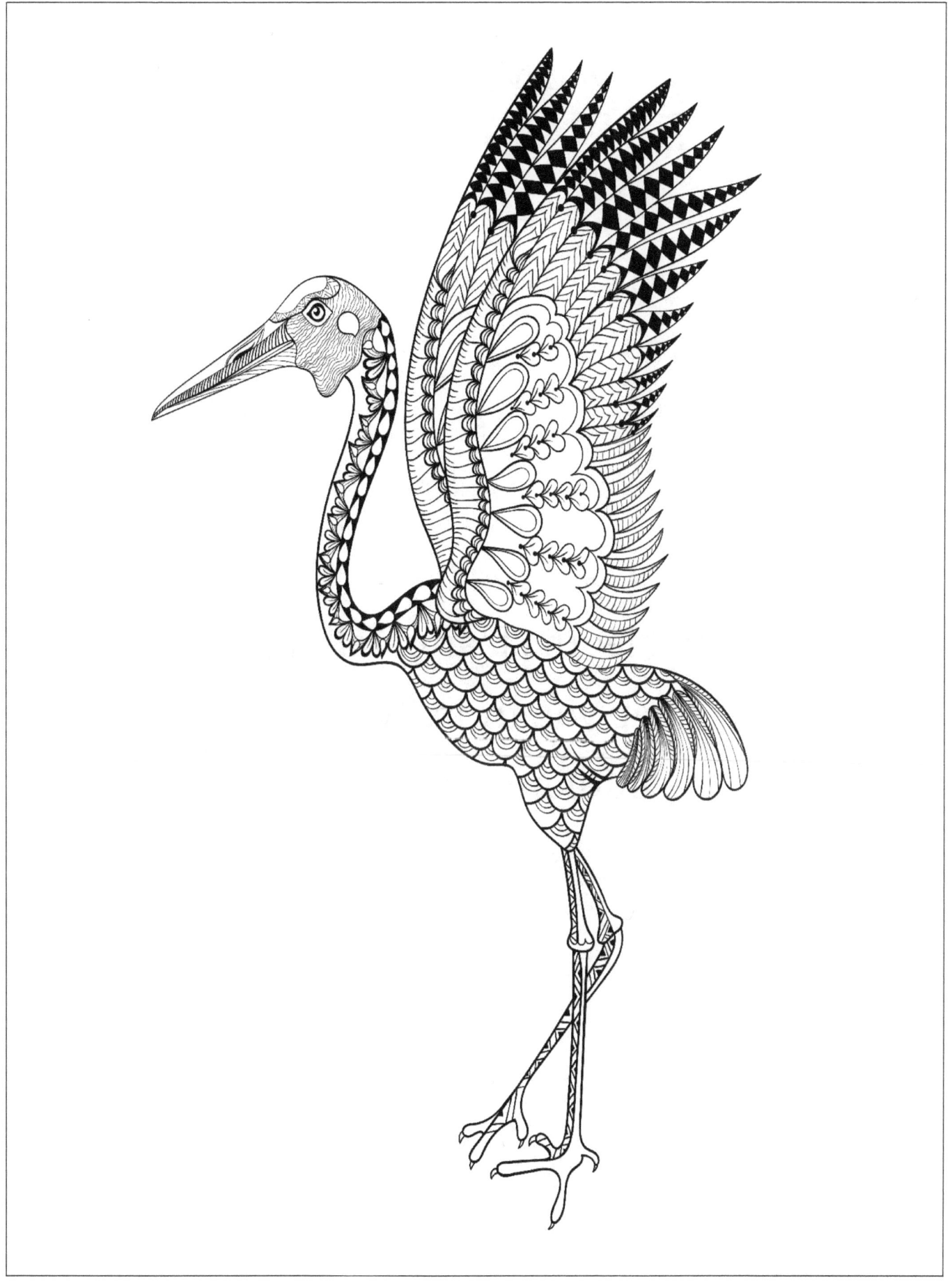

Level 3

Don't let the fear of falling,

keep you from flying.

- Author Unknown.

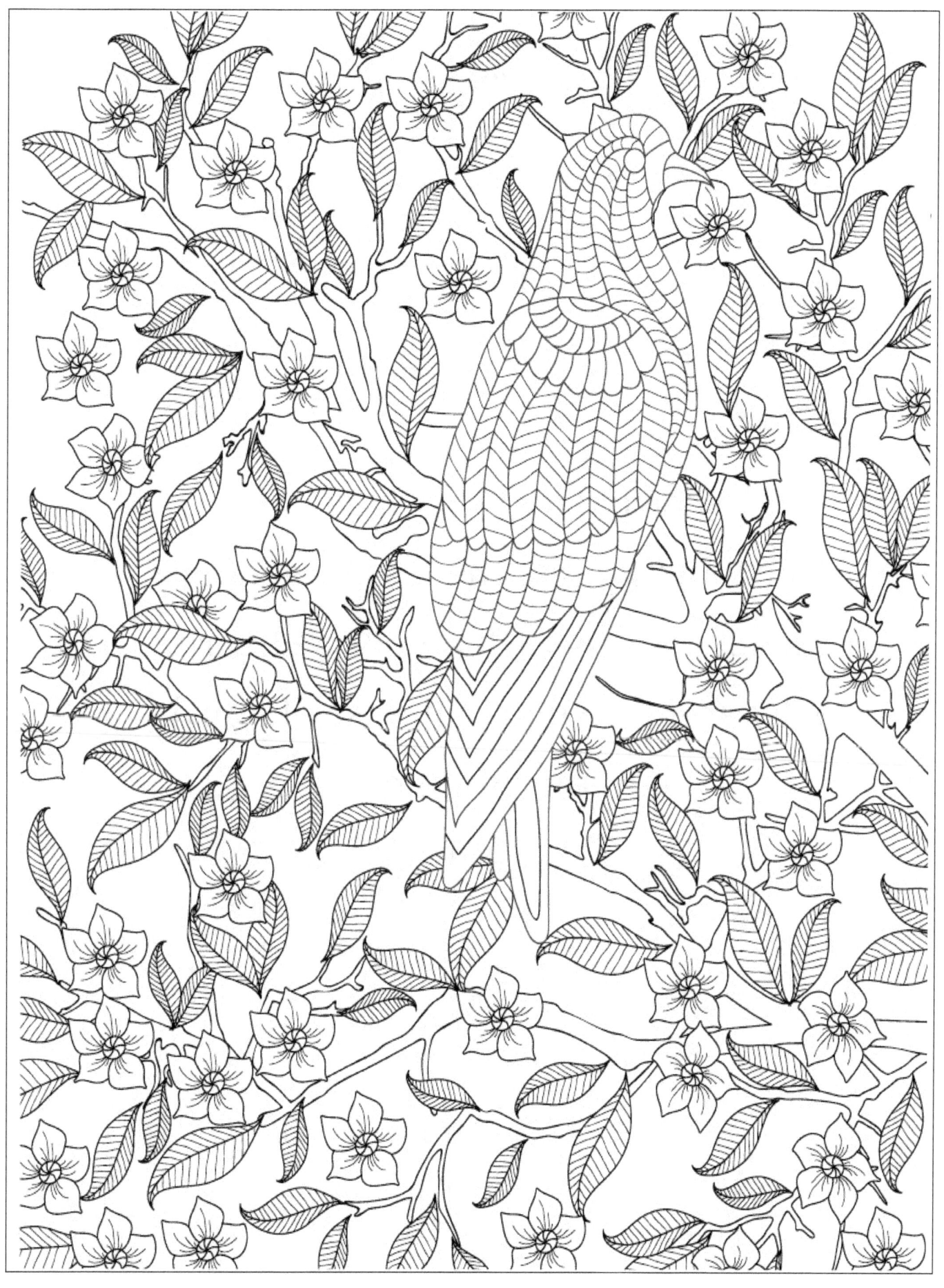

Level 3

A wise old owl sat on an oak;

the more he saw the less he spoke;

the less he spoke the more he heard.

Why arent we like that wise old bird.

– Author Unknown

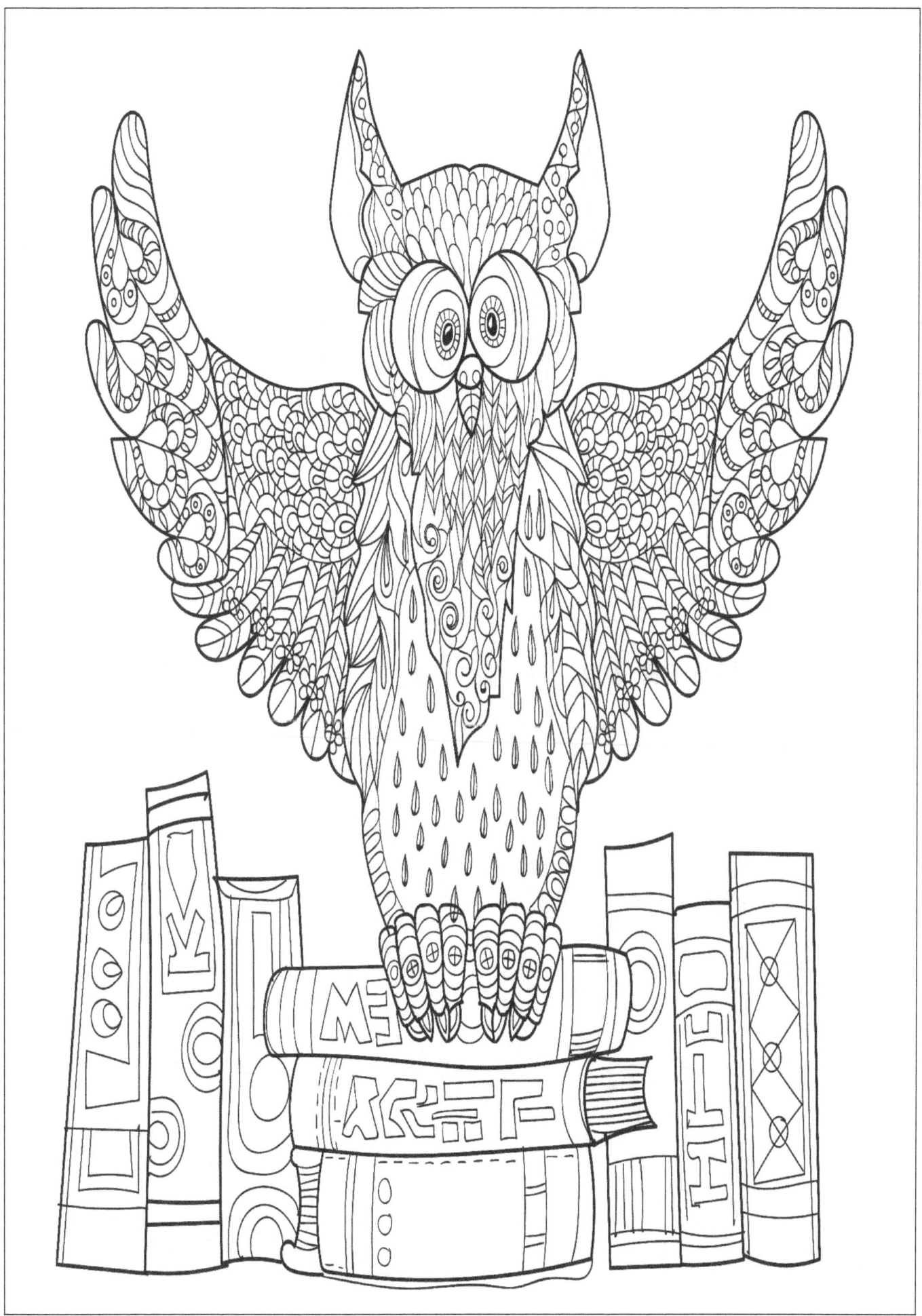

Level 2

Sometimes you gotta fall before you fly.

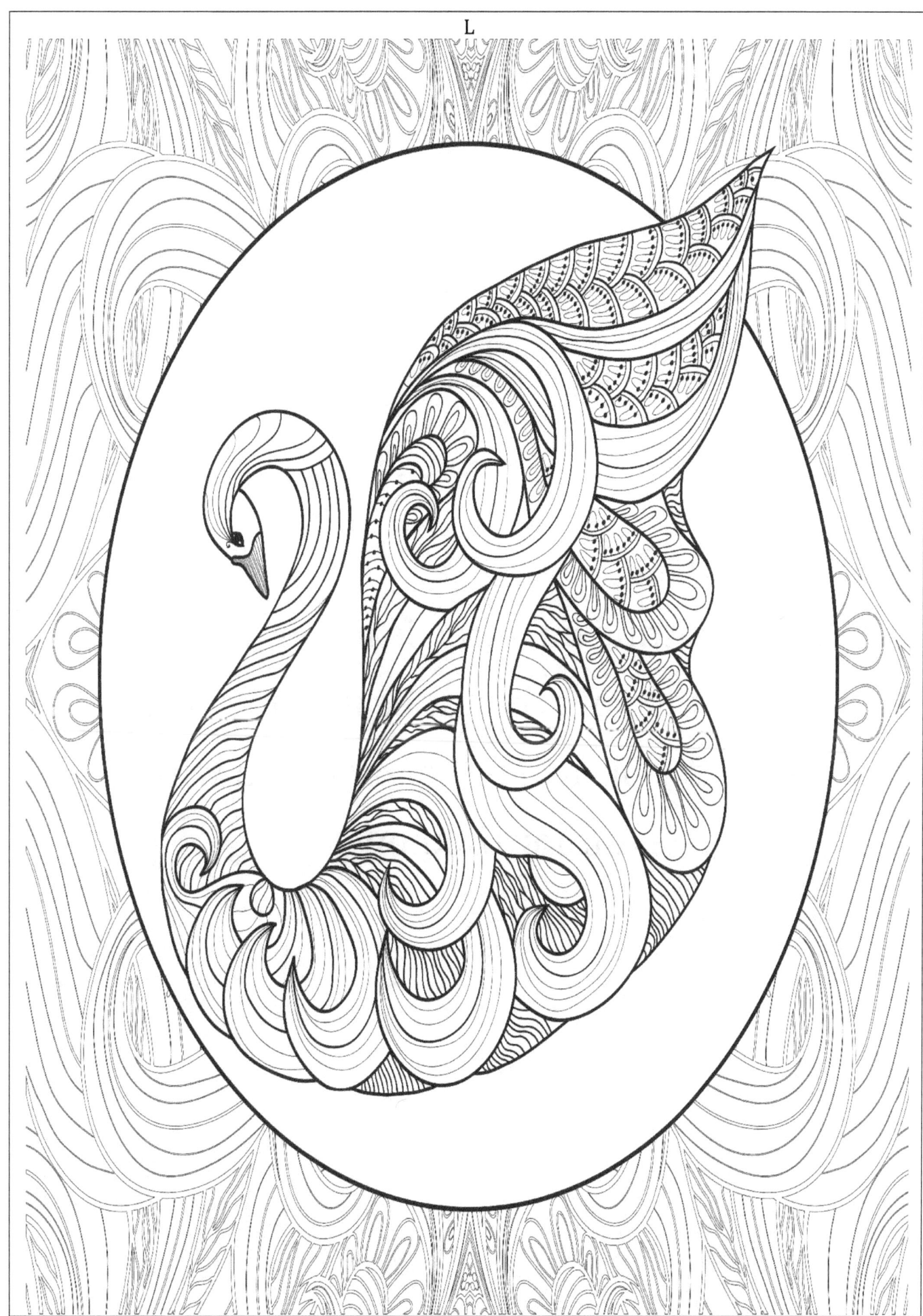

Level 2

A bird sitting on a tree is never afraid
of the branch breaking, because her trust
is not on the branch but on her own wings.
- Author Unknown.

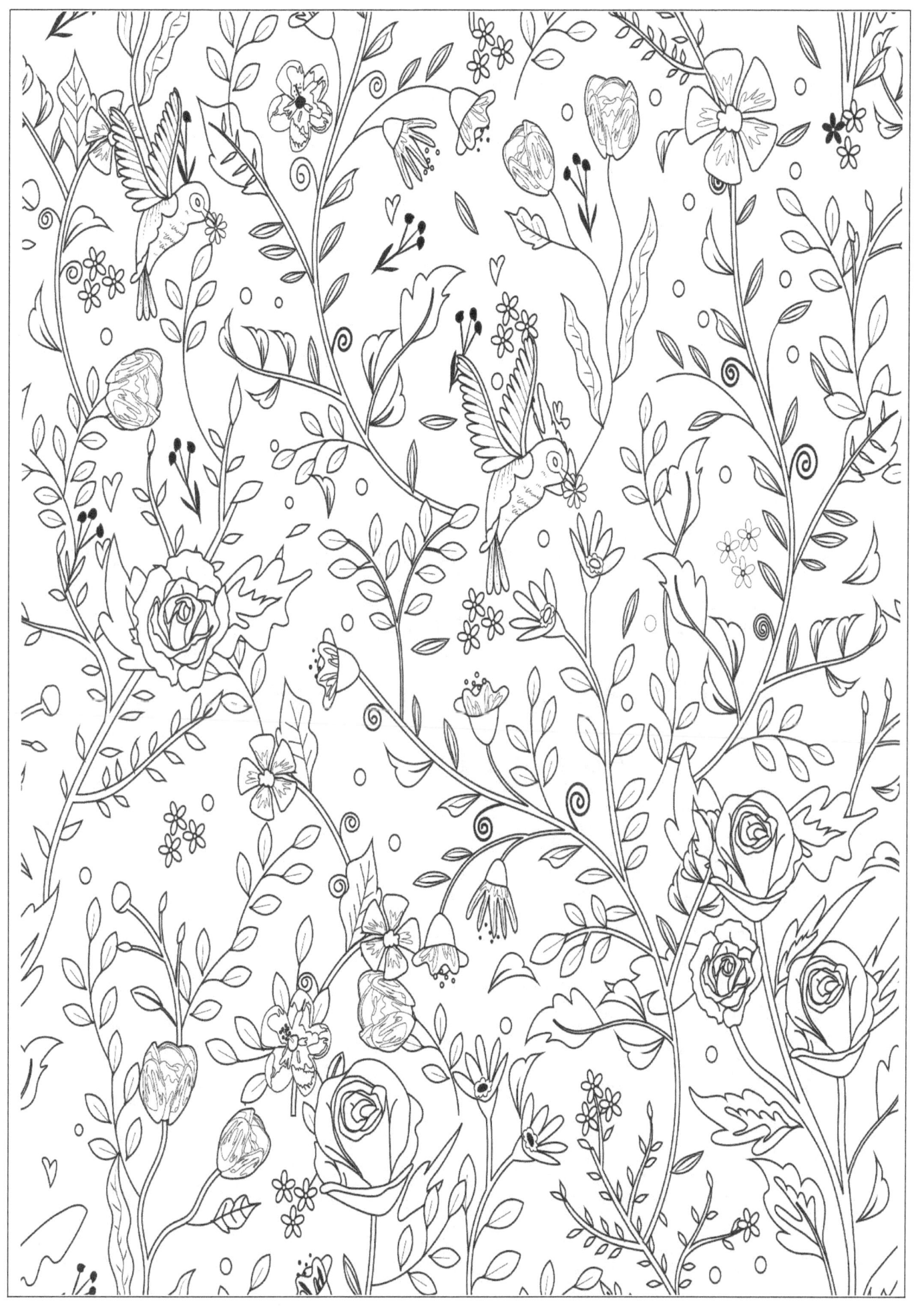

Level 2

Always be yourself.

Unless you can be a peacock,

then always be a peacock.

- Author Unknown.

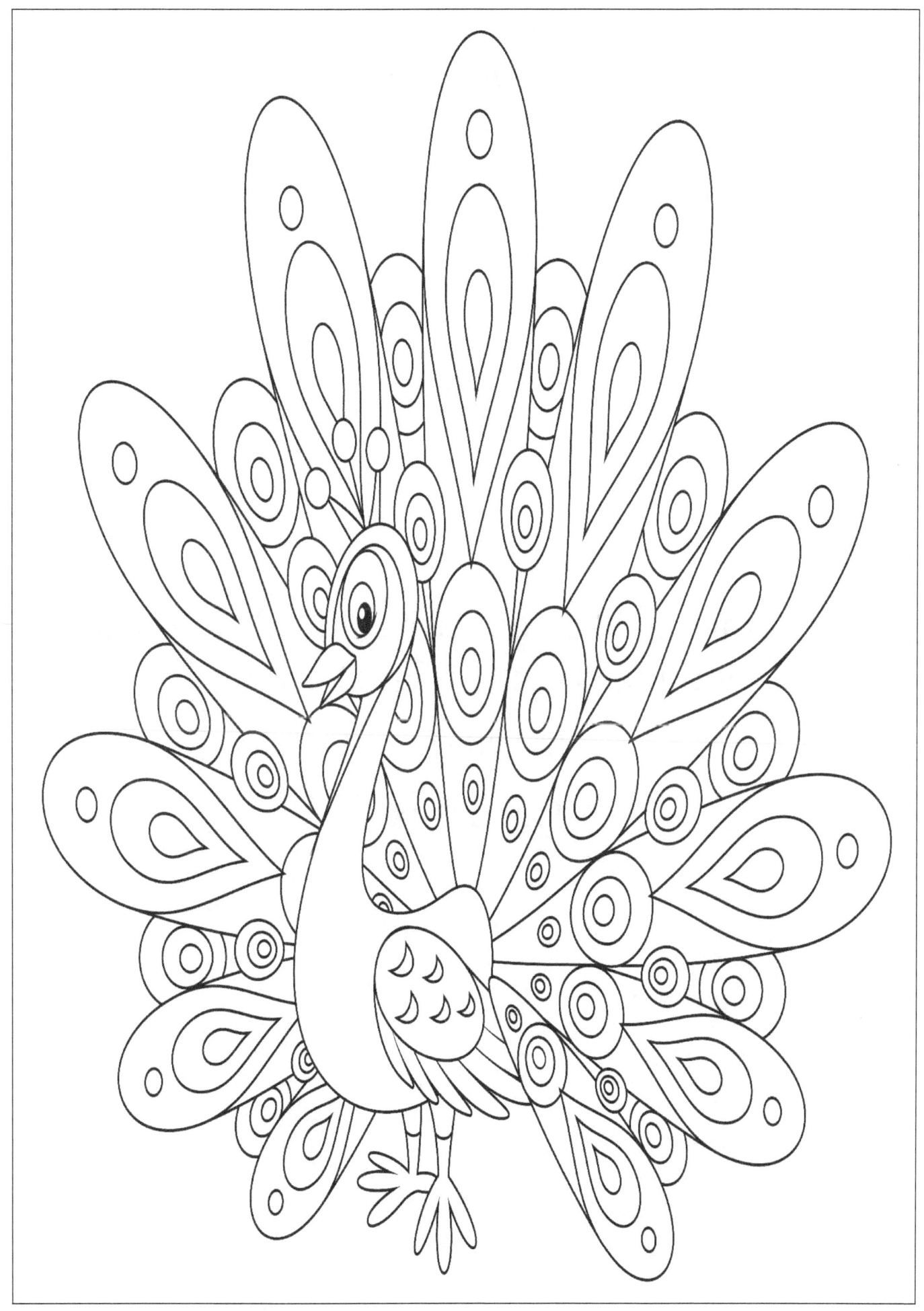

Level 2

Unless someone like you cares a whole awful lot, nothing is going to get better.

It's NOT.

- The Lorax

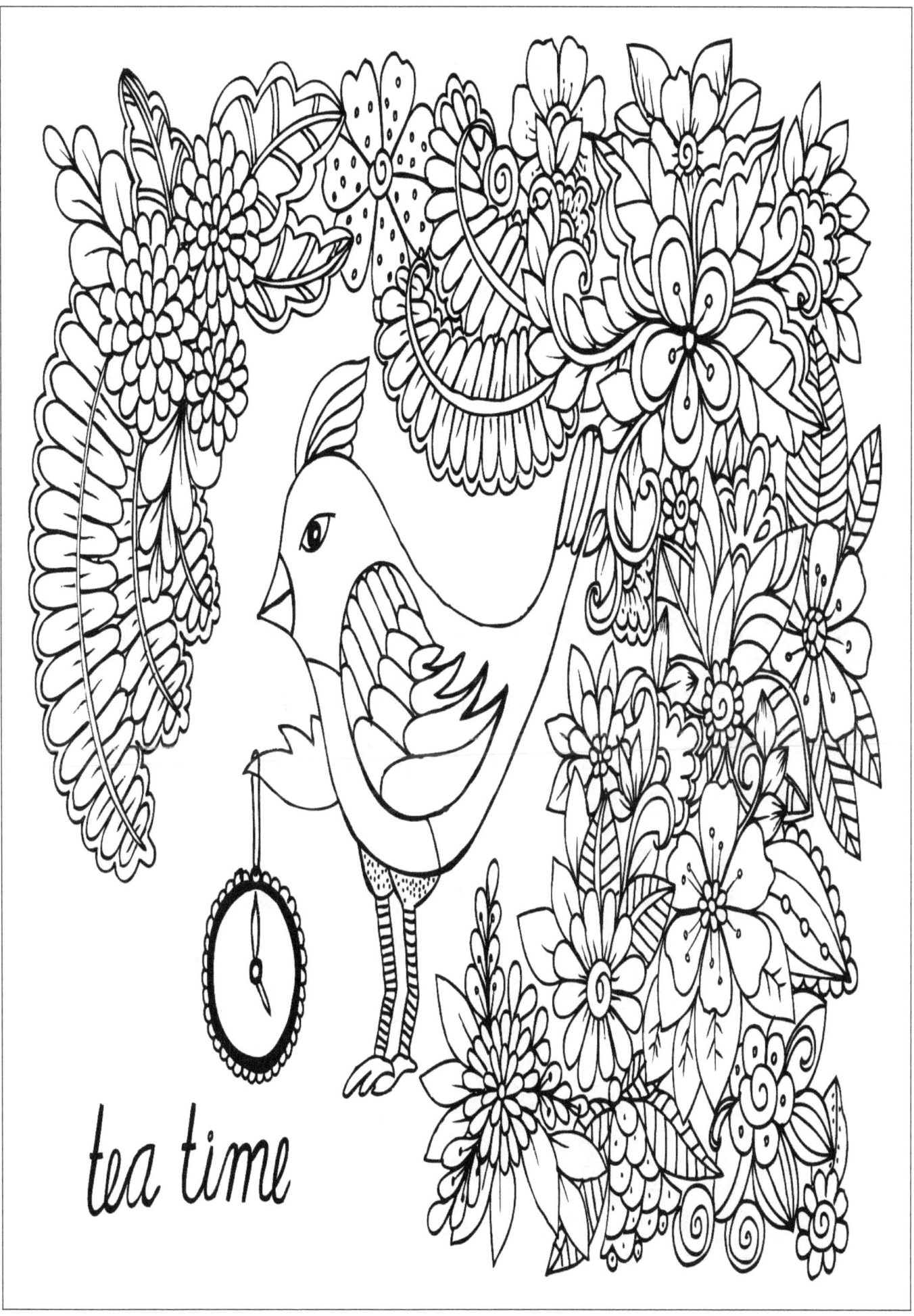

Level 3

Never interrupt someone doing something
you said couldn't be done.

- Amilia Earhart

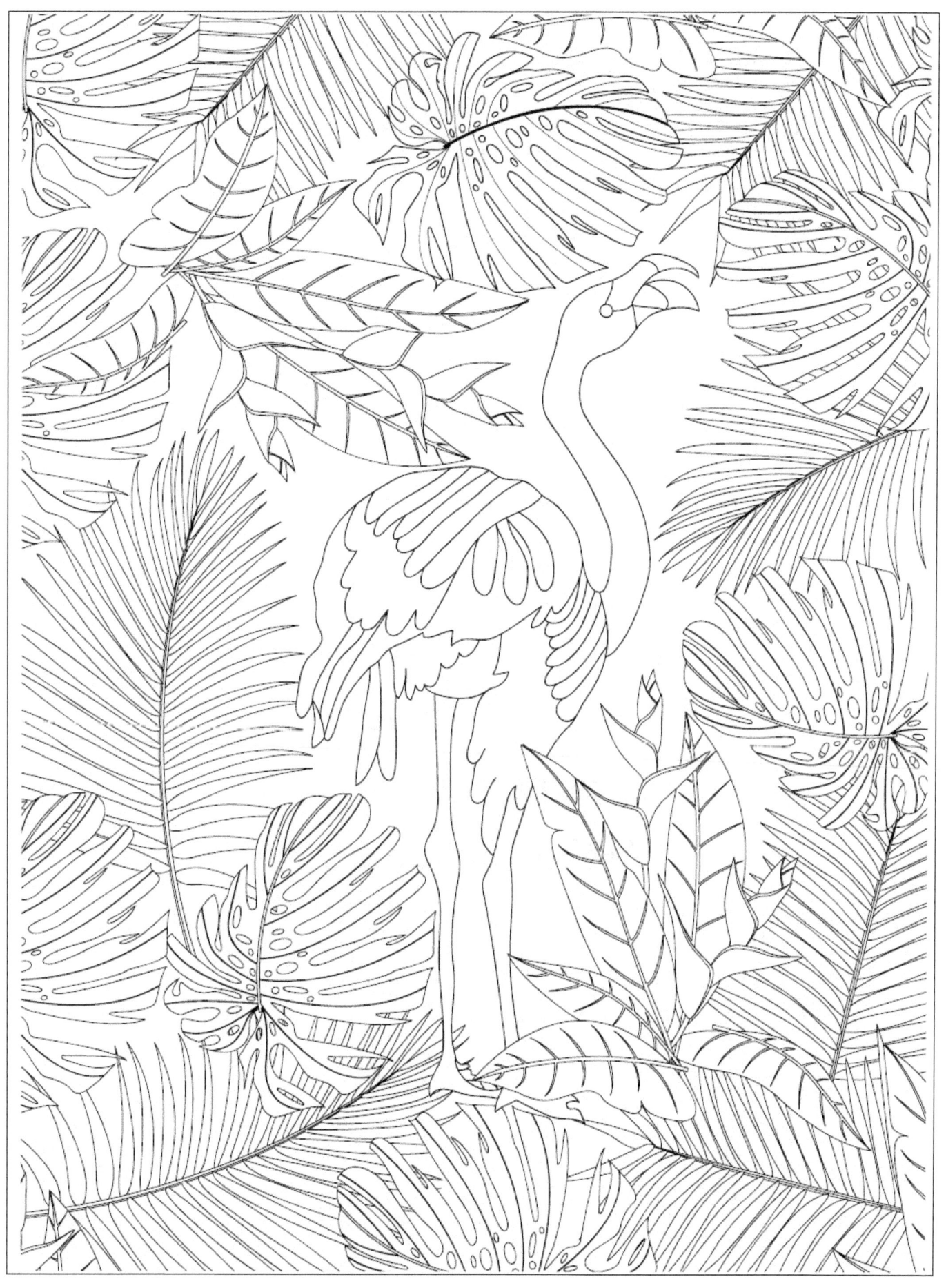

Level 3

Become like a bird,

Expand your wings,

Learn new things,

And fly as high as you can.

- Author Unknown

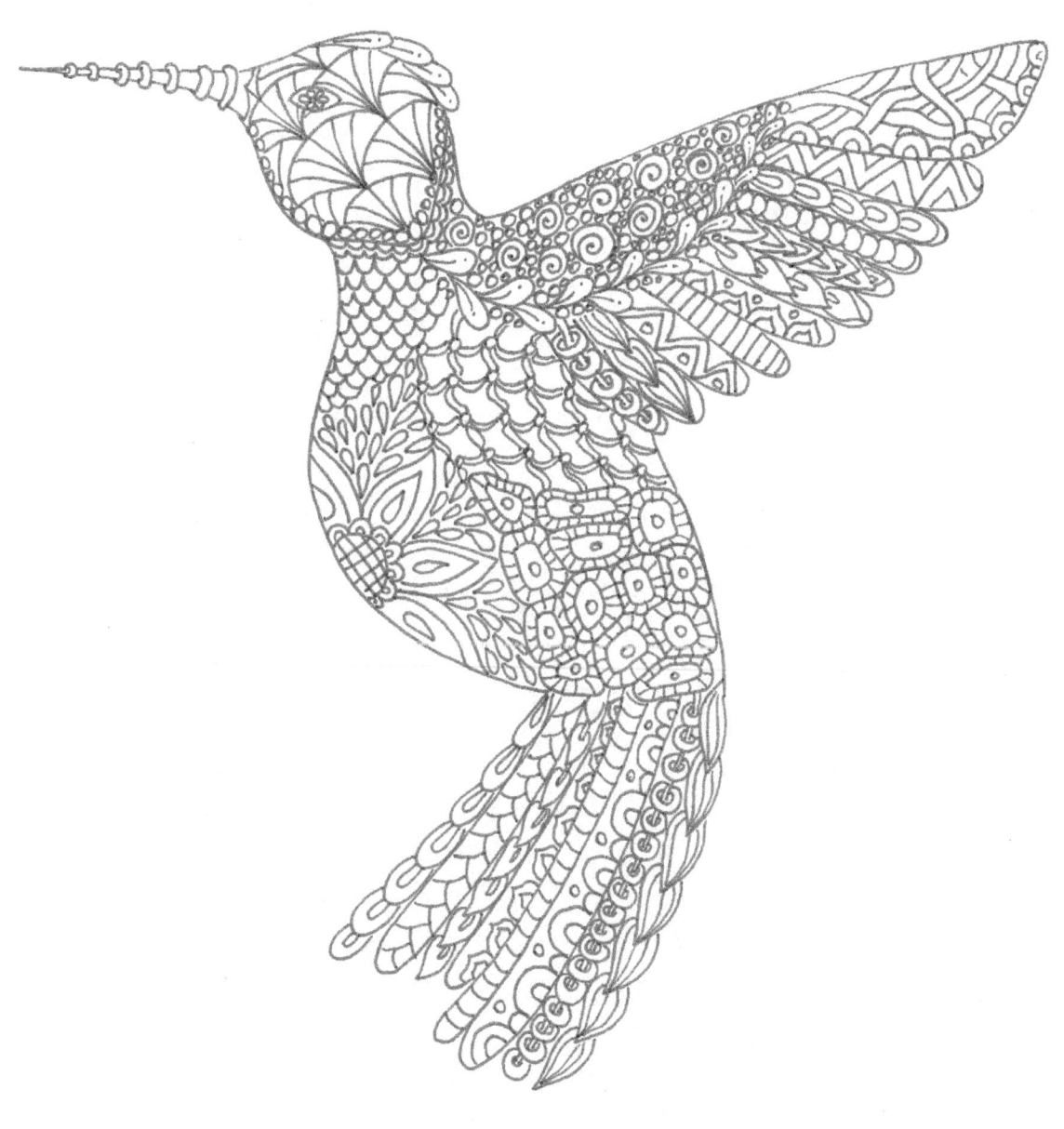

Level 2

Gravity sucks.

I want to fly.

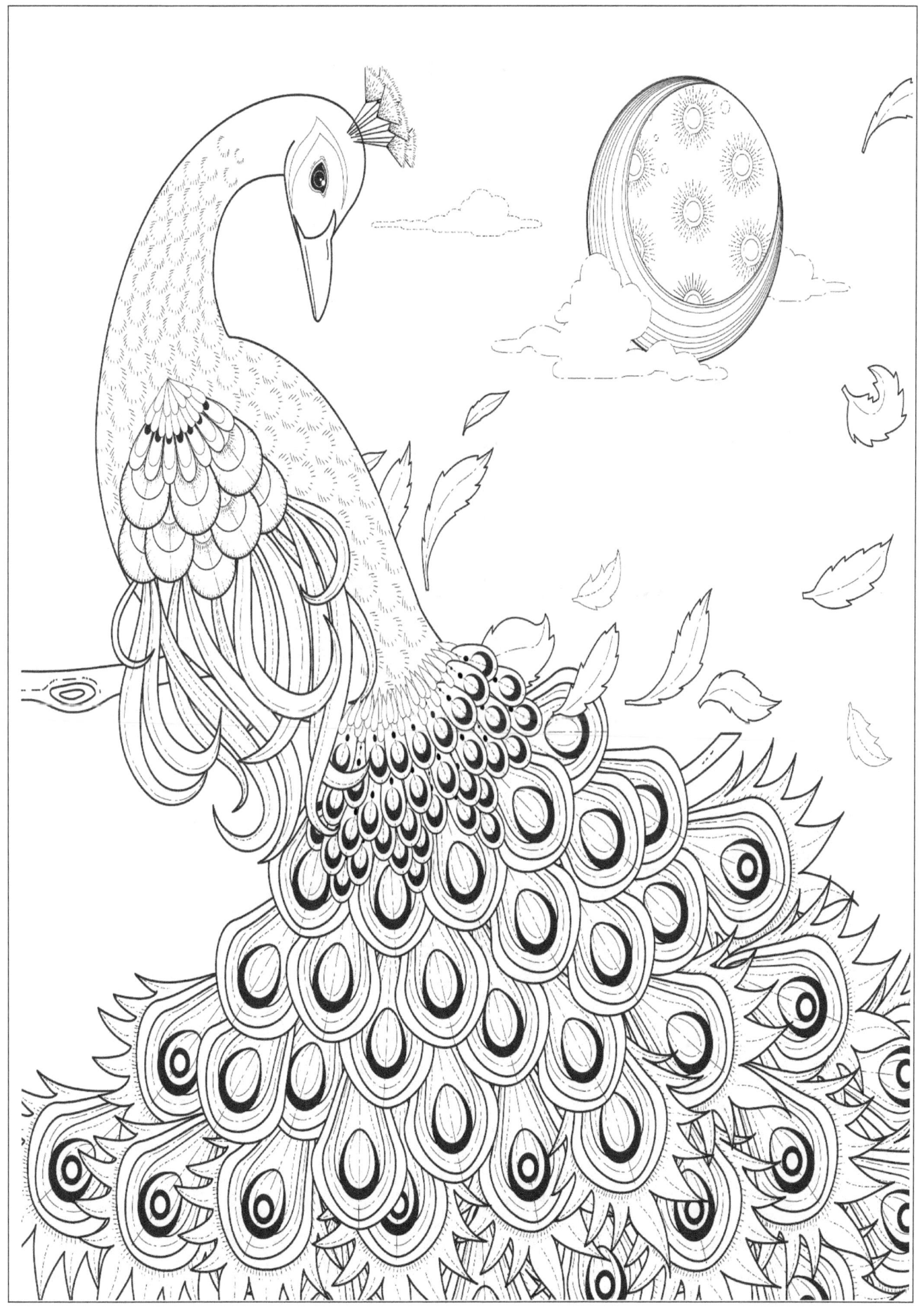

Level 3

Faith is the bird that sings when the

dawn is still dark.

- Rabindranath Tagore

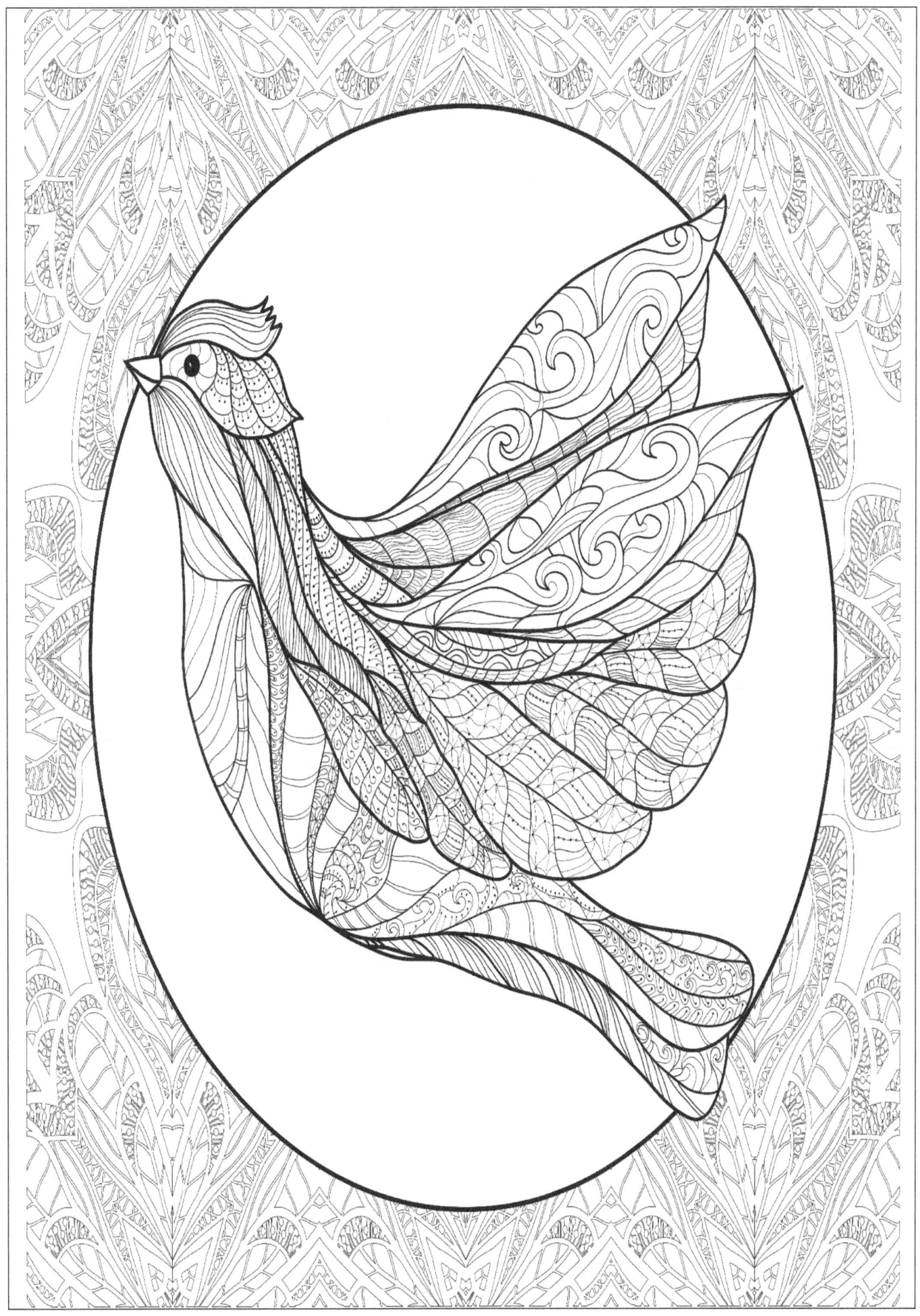

Level 1

I think we consider too much the
good luck of the early bird,
and not enough the bad luck of the early worm.
- Franklin D.Roosevelt

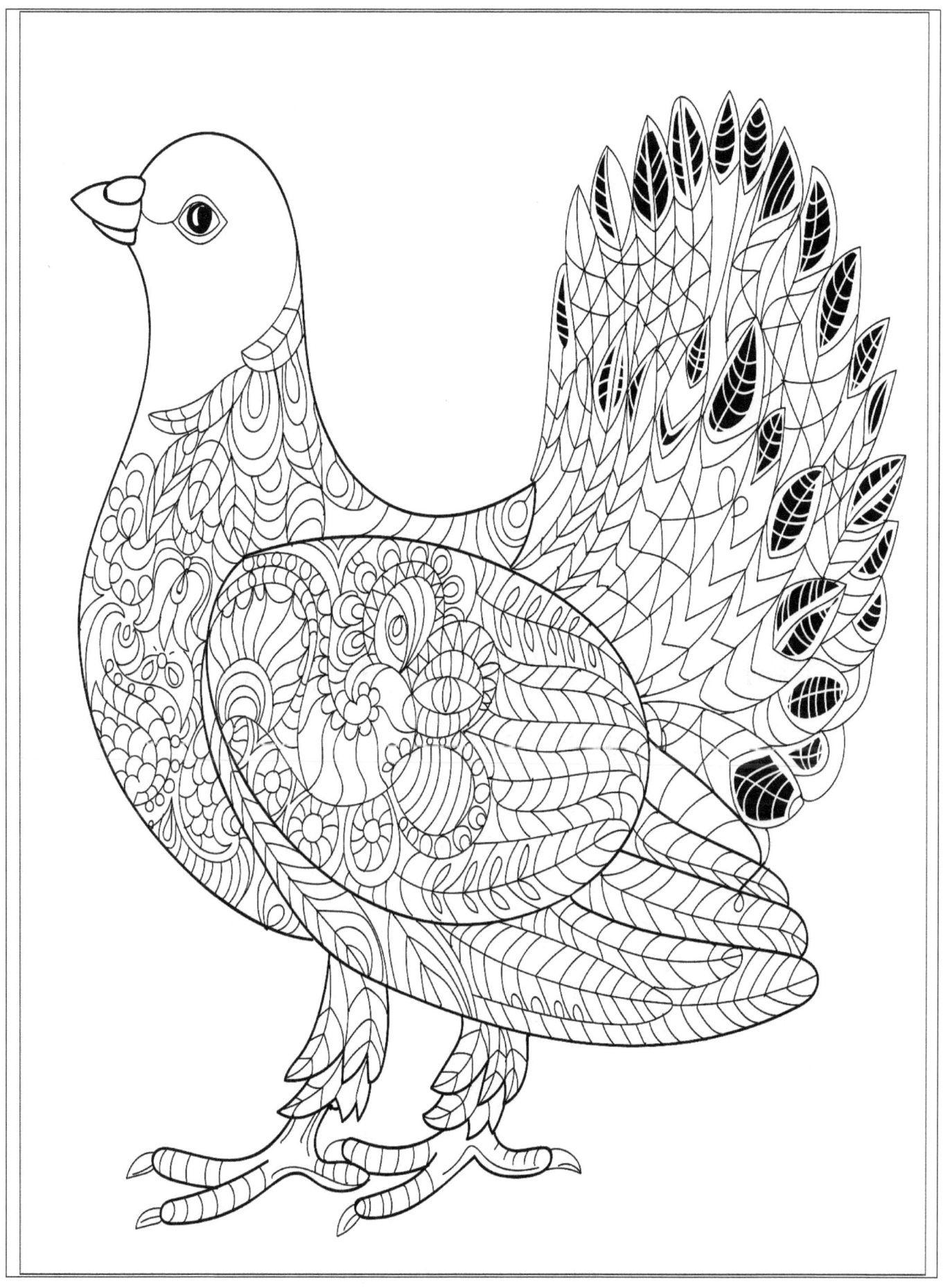

Level 3

Birds of a feather flock together.

-Author unknown.

.

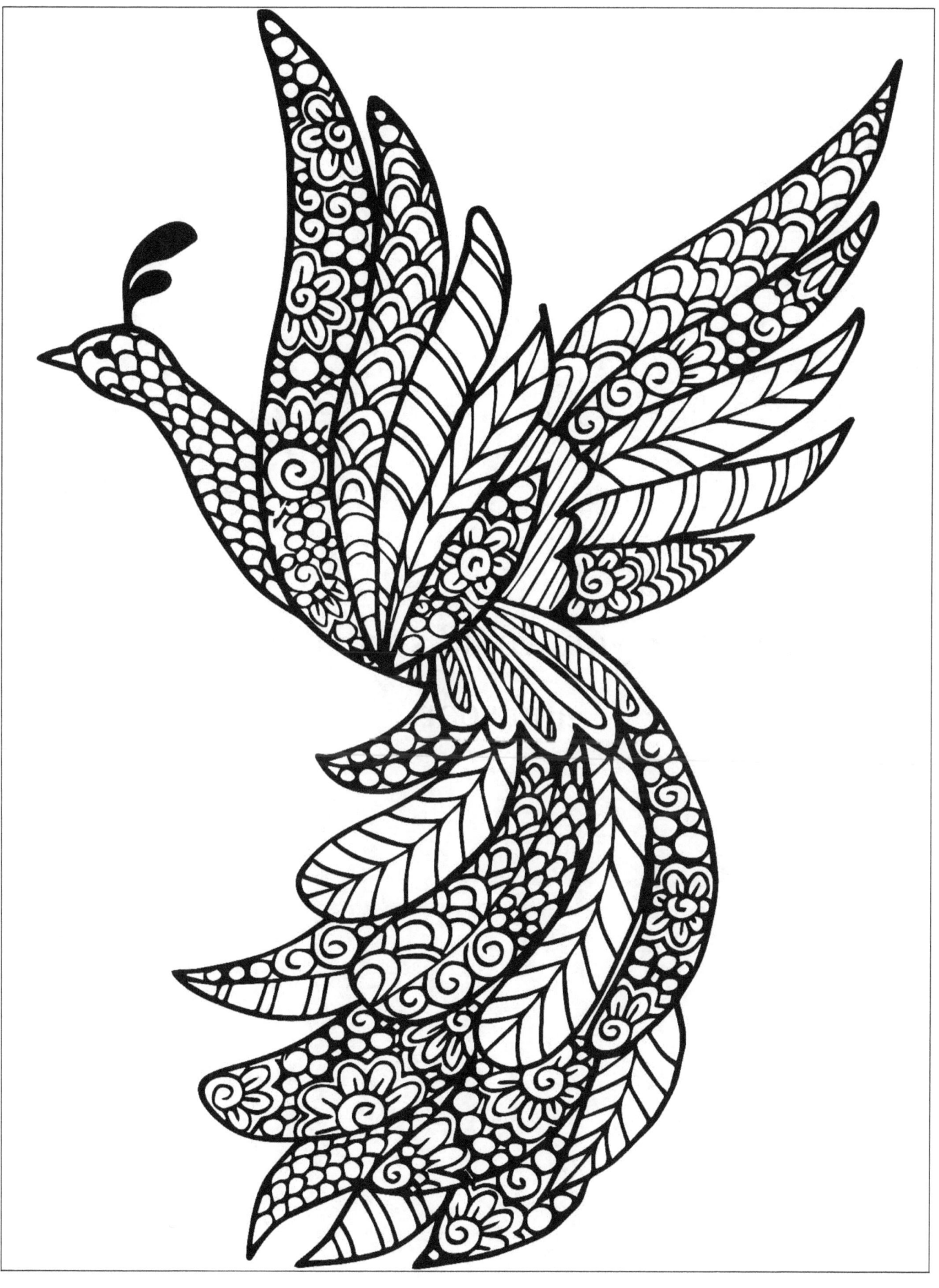

Level 3

I always knew you would spread your wings
and soar.

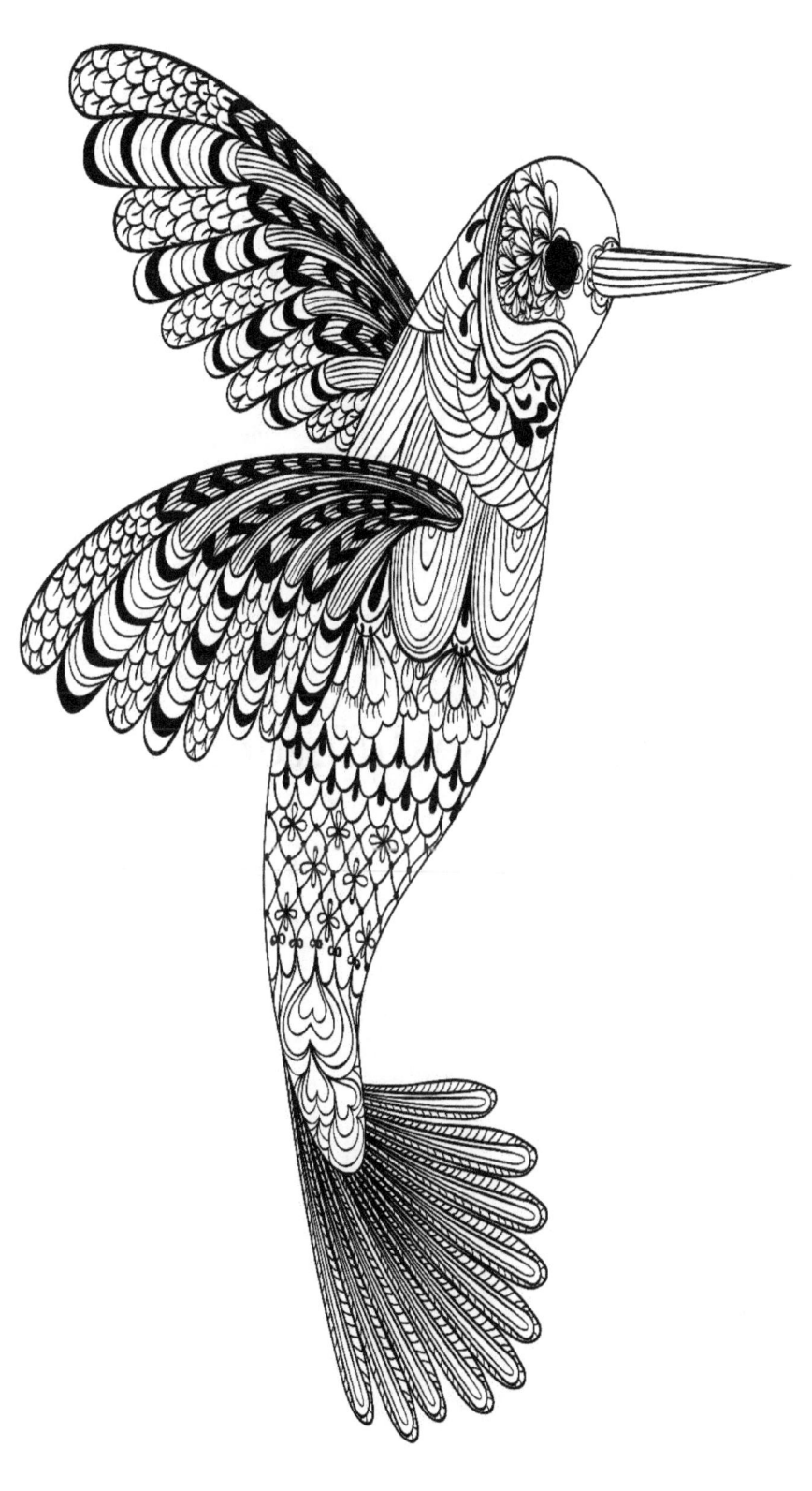

Level 2

Dare to be different.

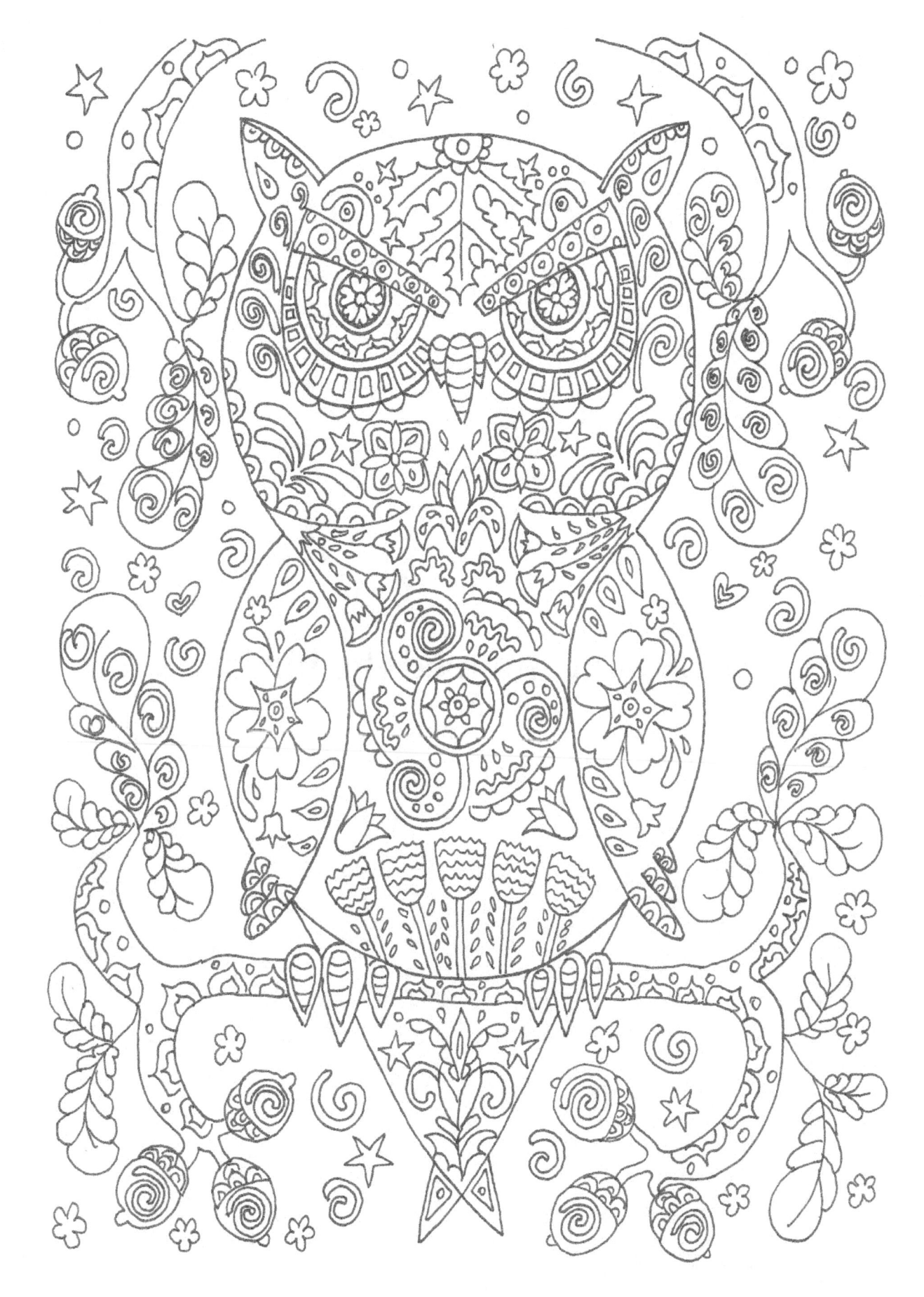

Level 2

Keep calm and feed the birds.

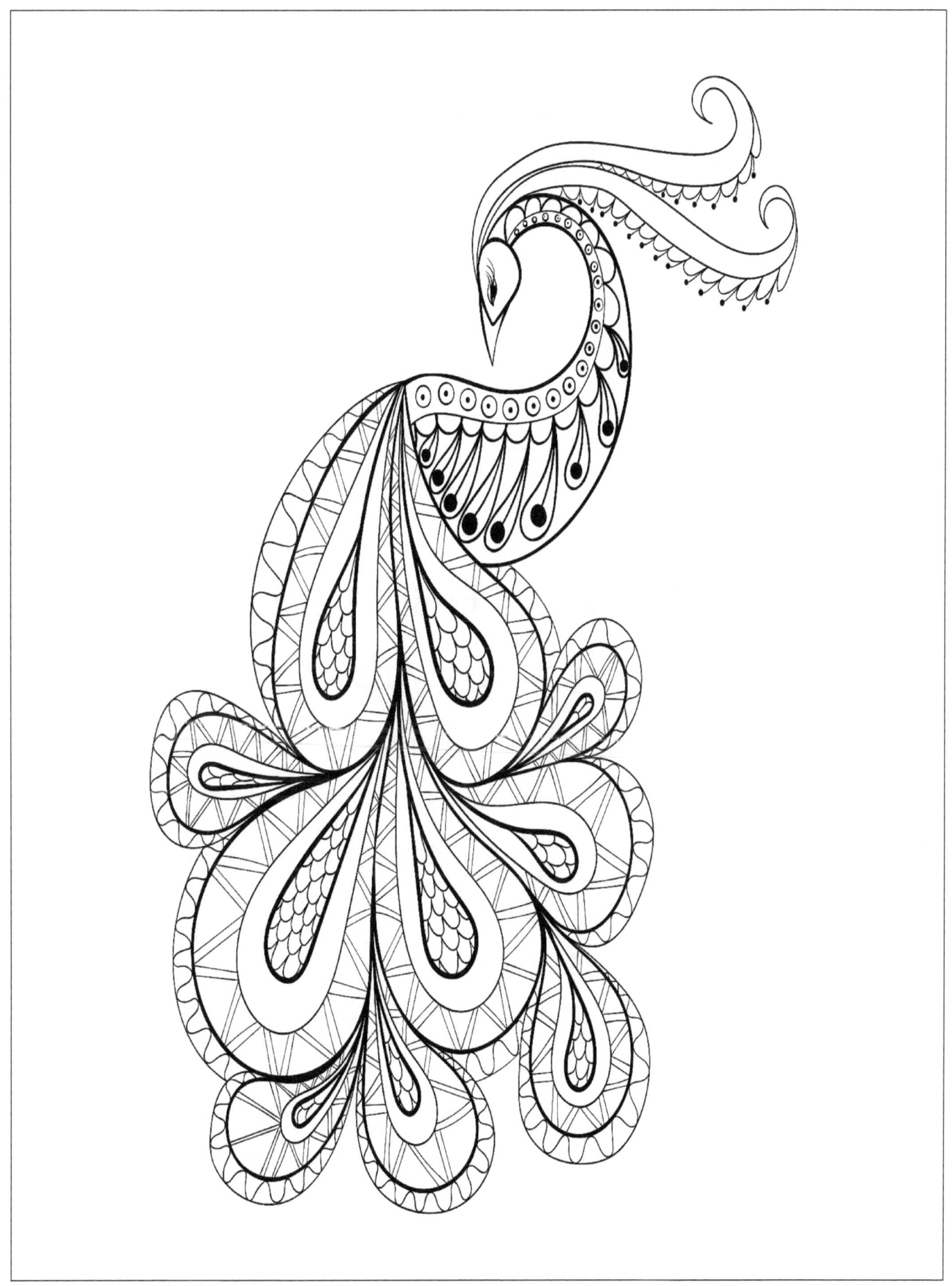

Level 3

No bird soars too high if he soars
with his own wings.
- William Blake

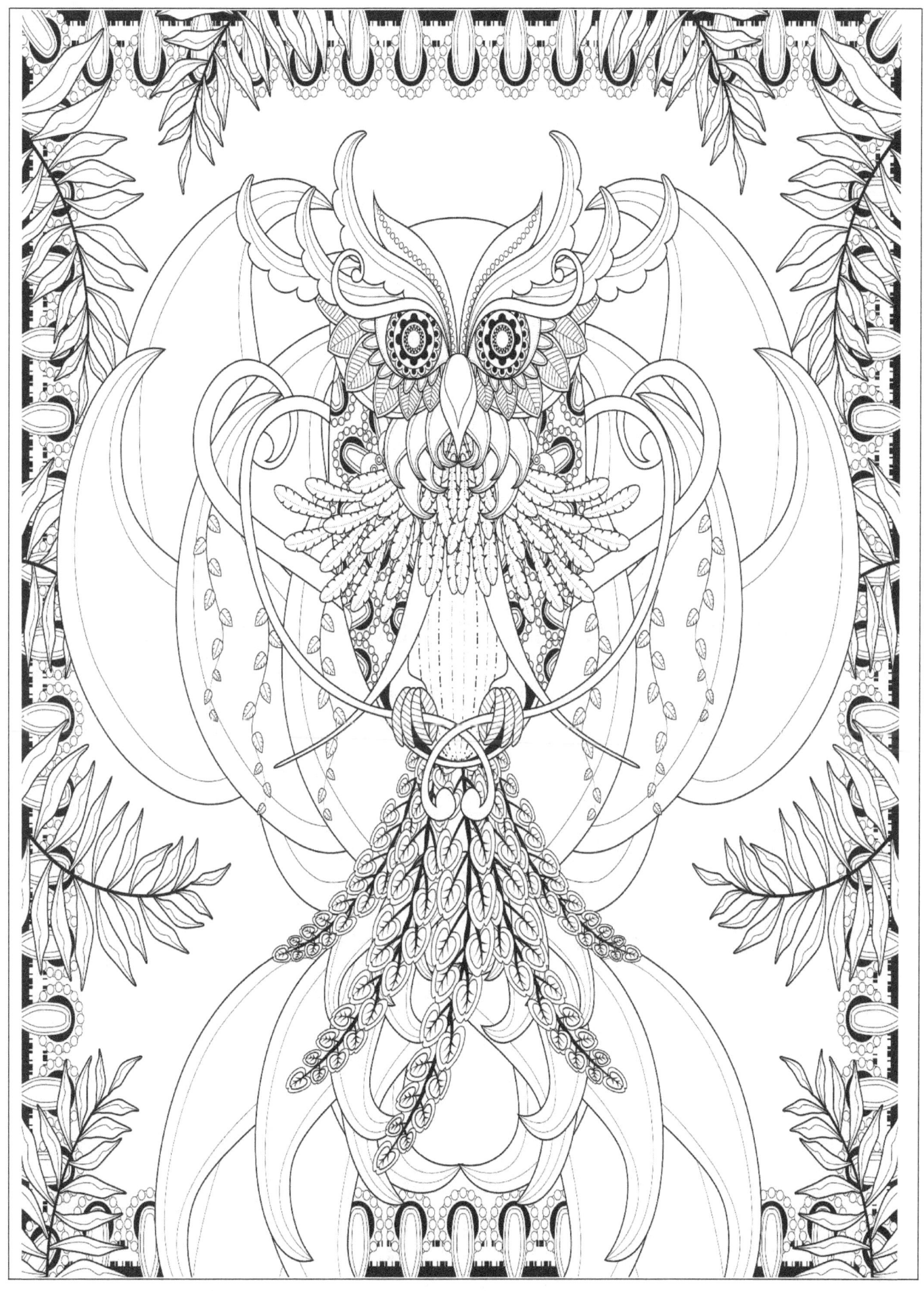

Level 3

Human beings are great in their own eyes,
but are not much in the eyes of Nature.
- Kensho Furuya

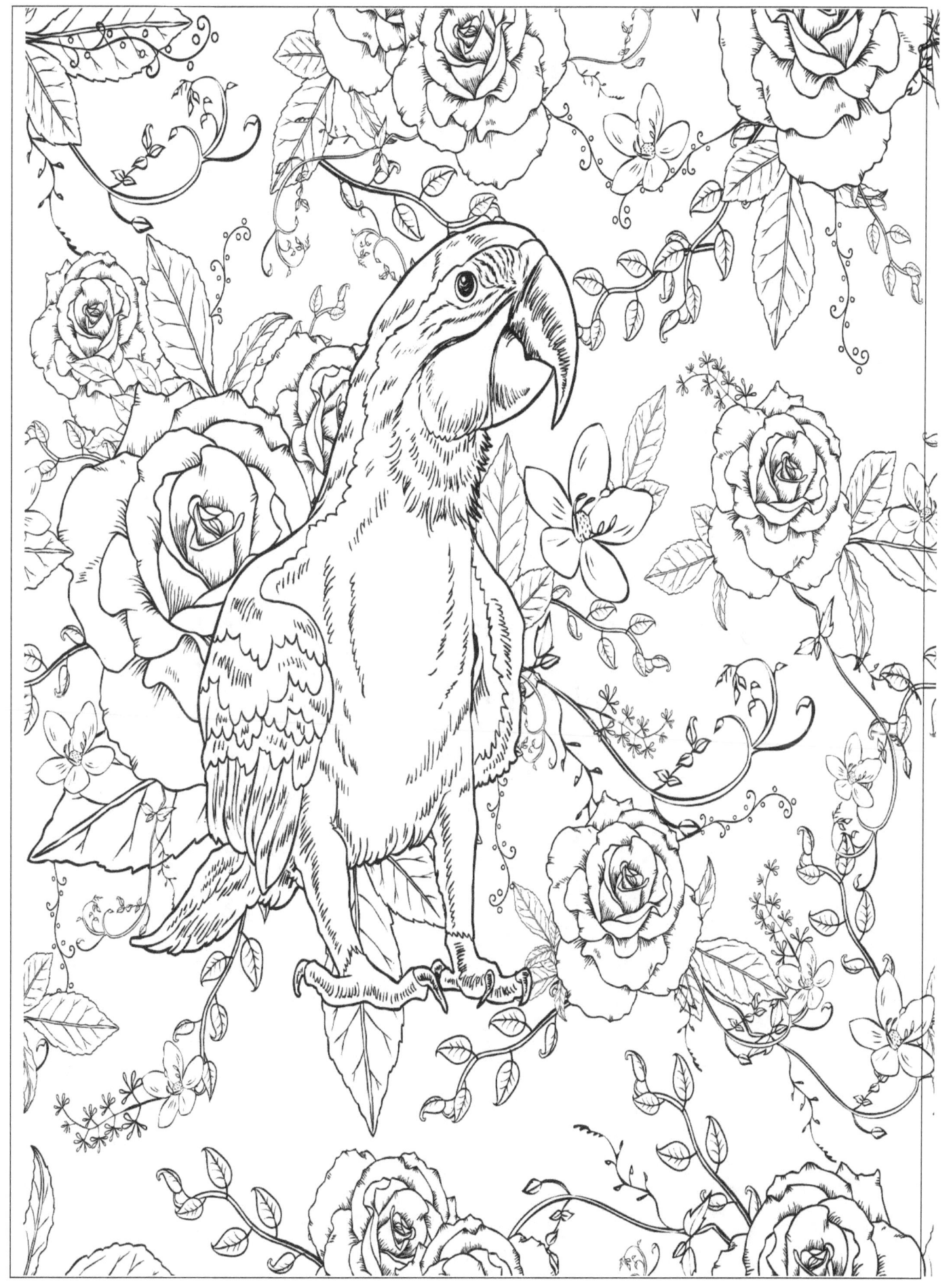

Level 3

It is not only fine feathers that
make fine birds.

-AESOP

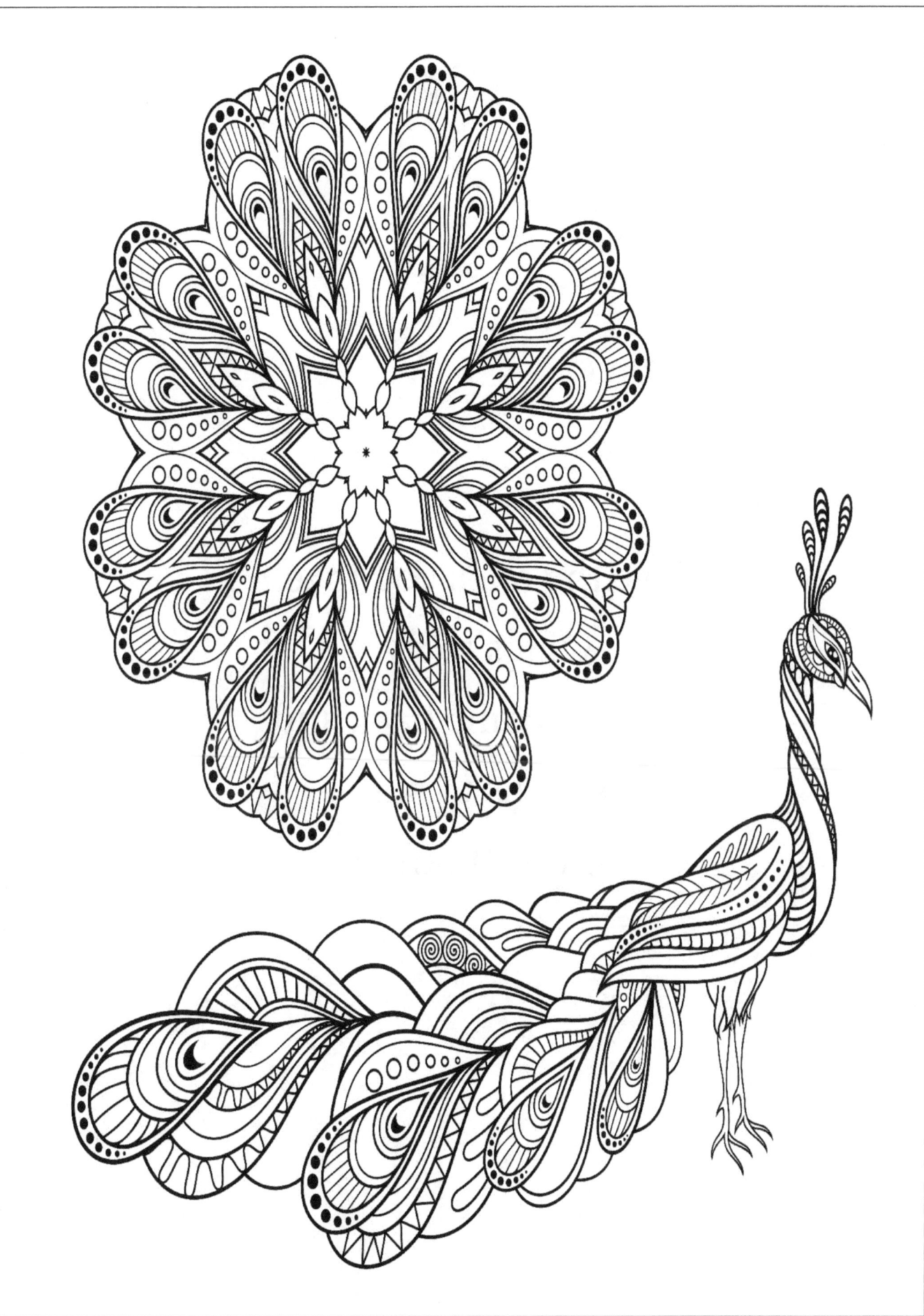

Level 3

Give the ones you love,

wings to fly,

roots to come back and

reasons to stay.

- Author Unknown.

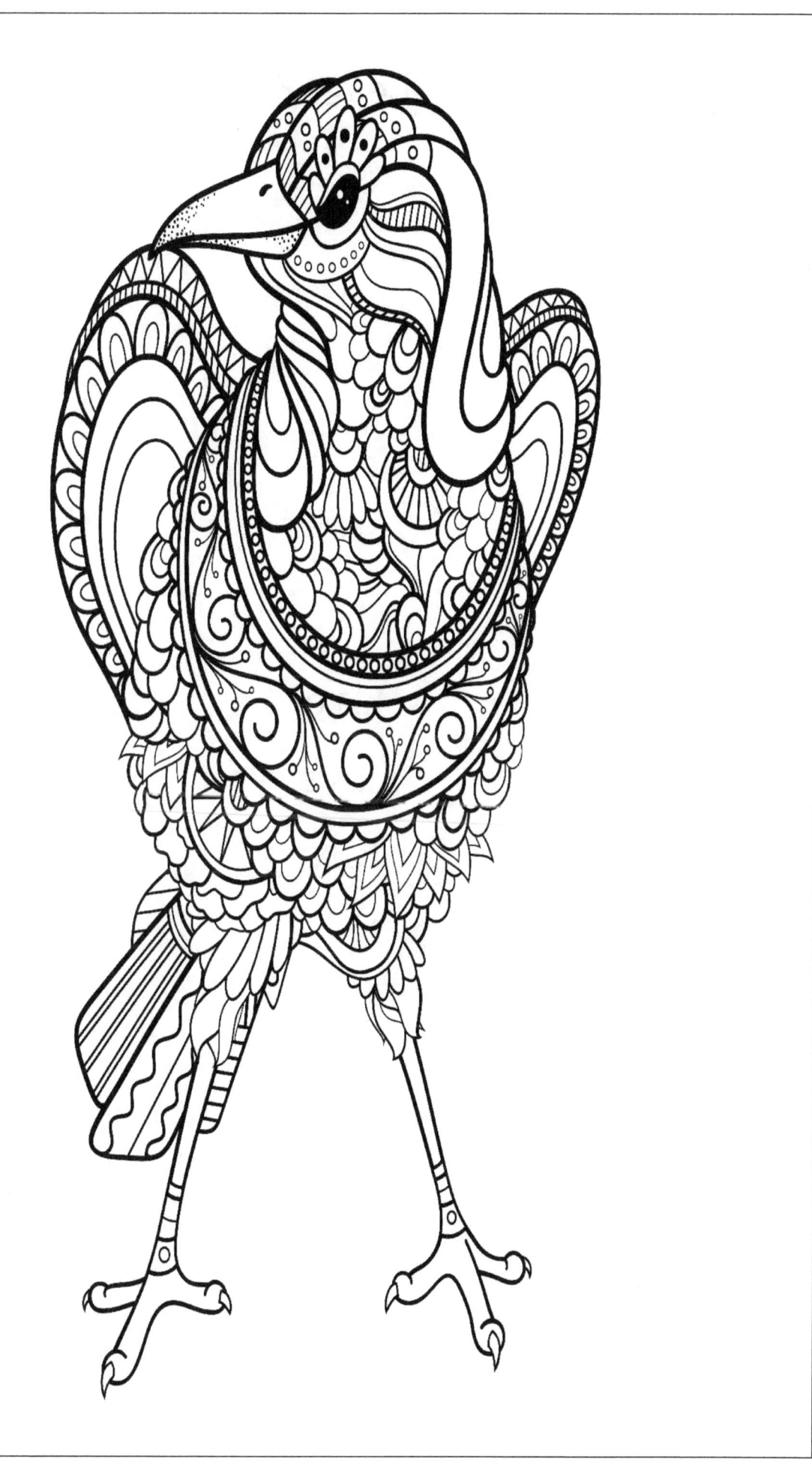

Level 3

Live.

Love.

Bird

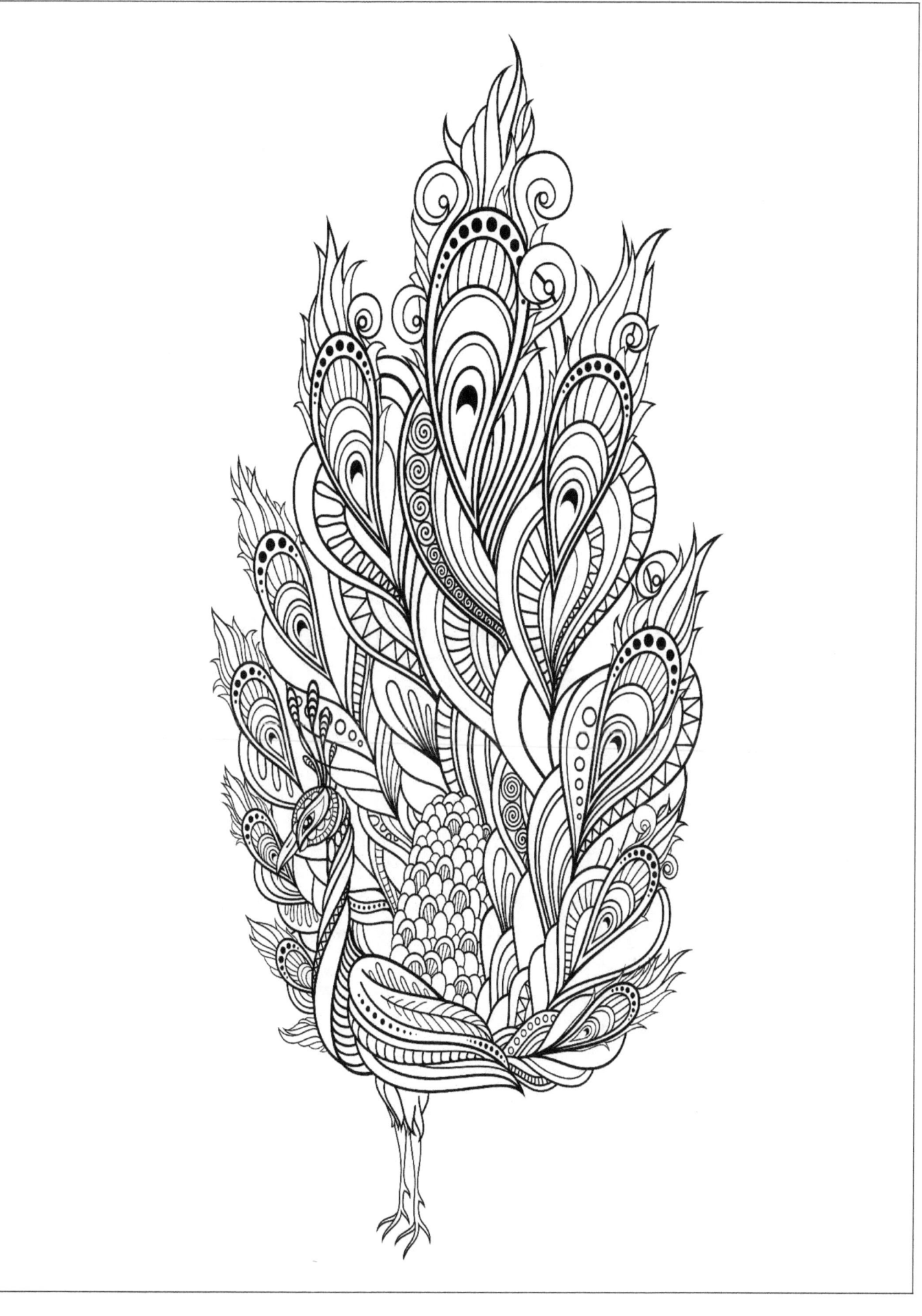

Level 2

All good things are wild and free.

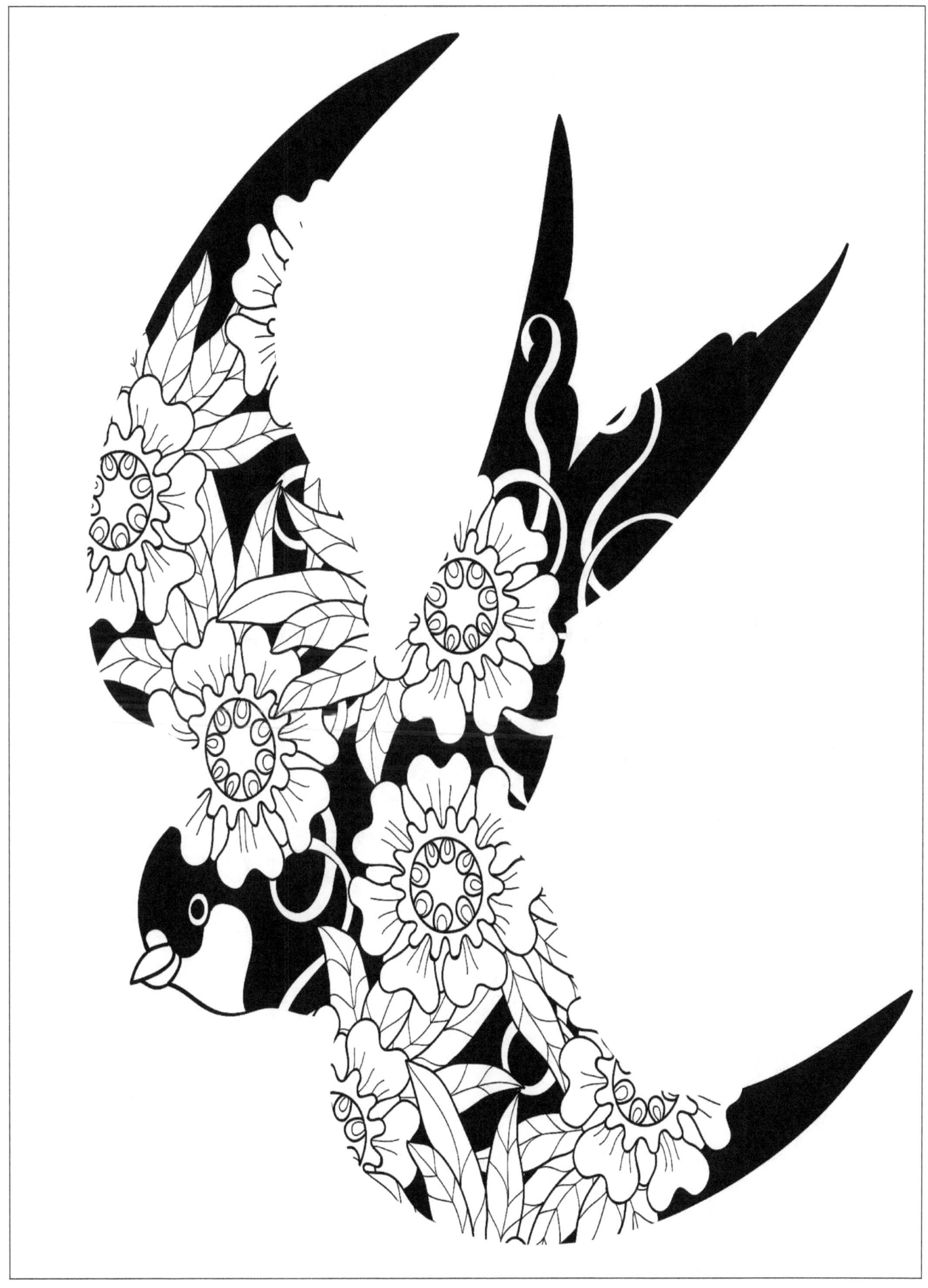

Level 2

Be your own kind of beautiful.

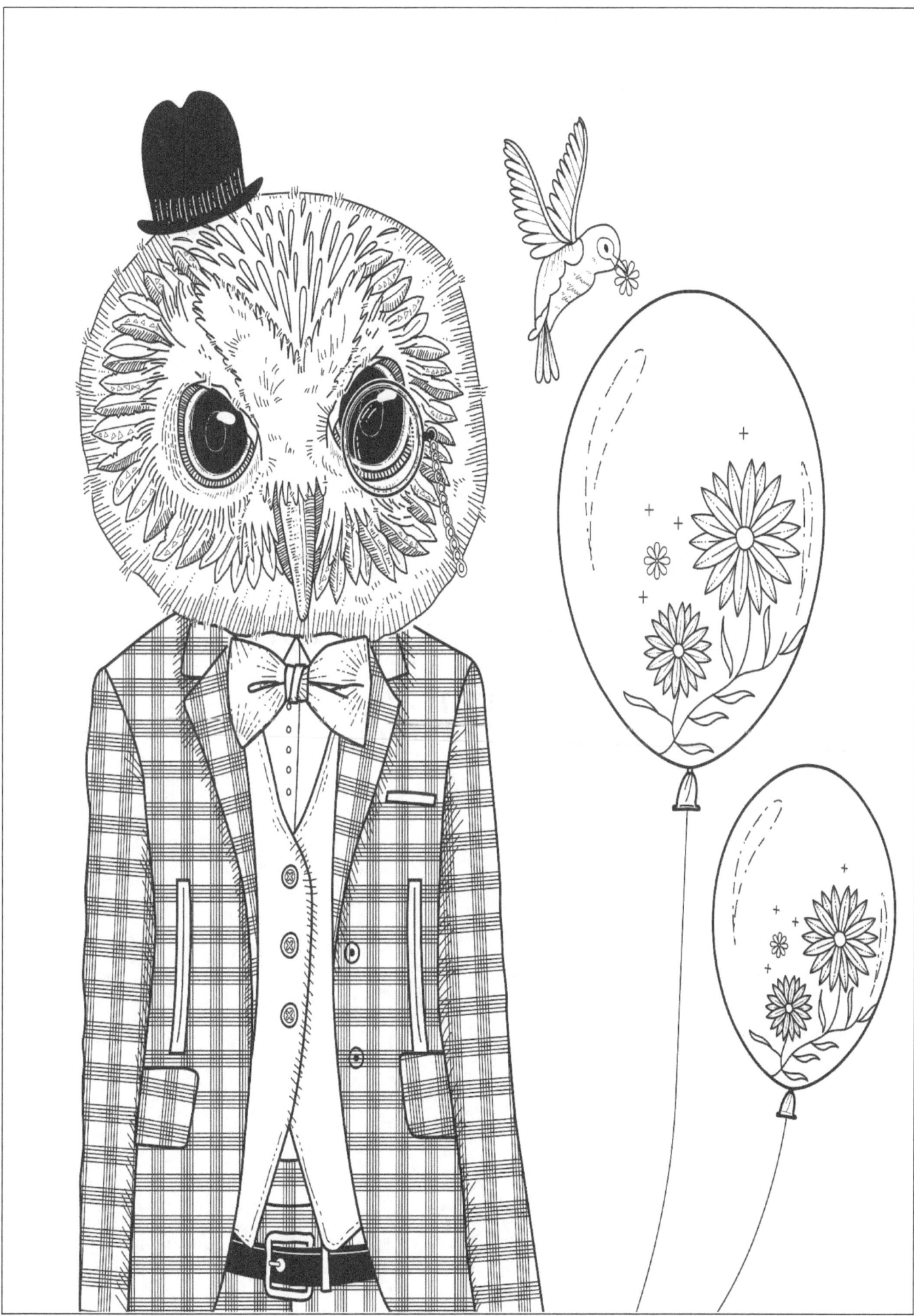

Level 2

You were born with wings,

why prefer to crawl through life.

- Rumi

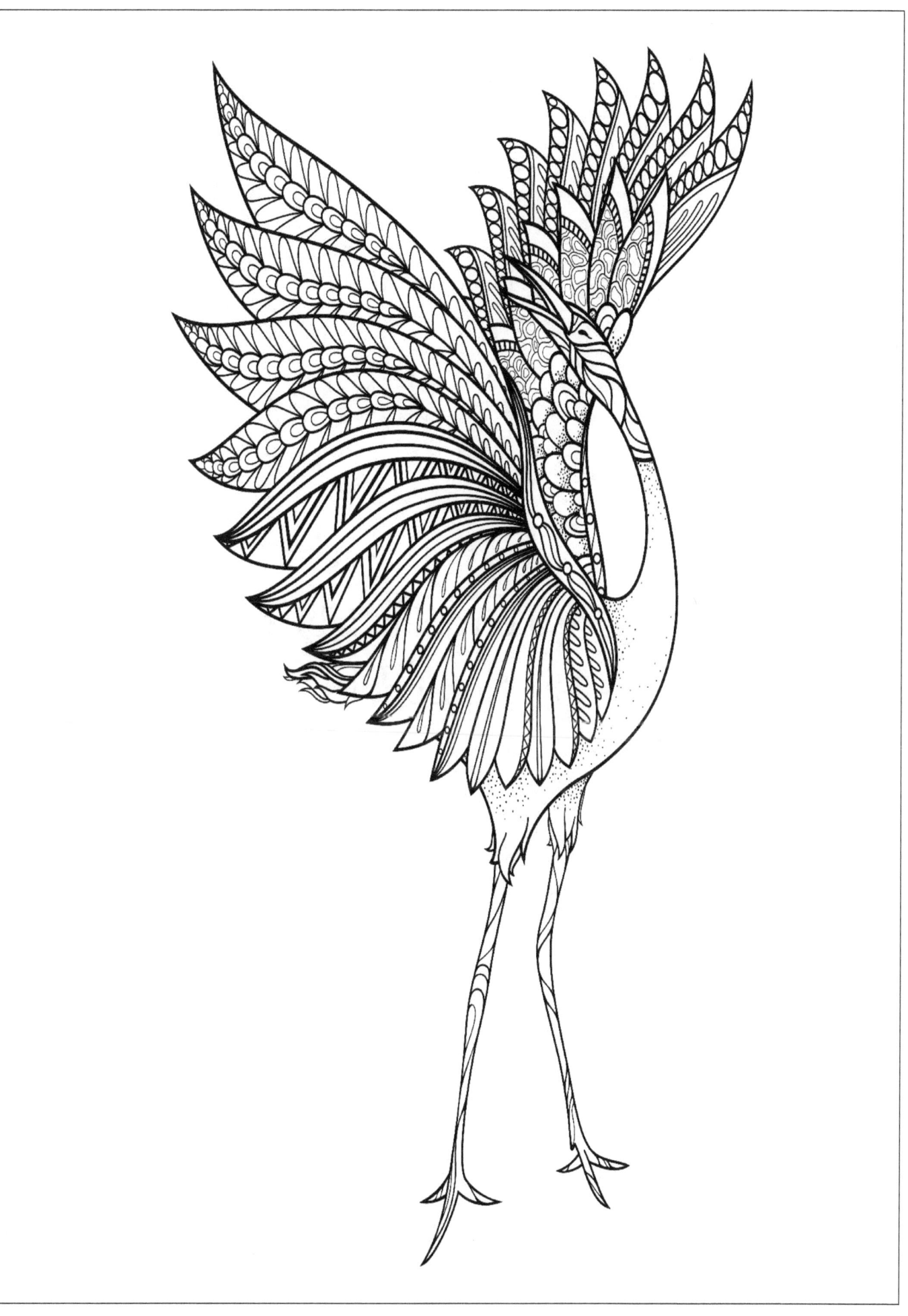

Level 2

If you're a bird, I'm a bird.

- The Notebook

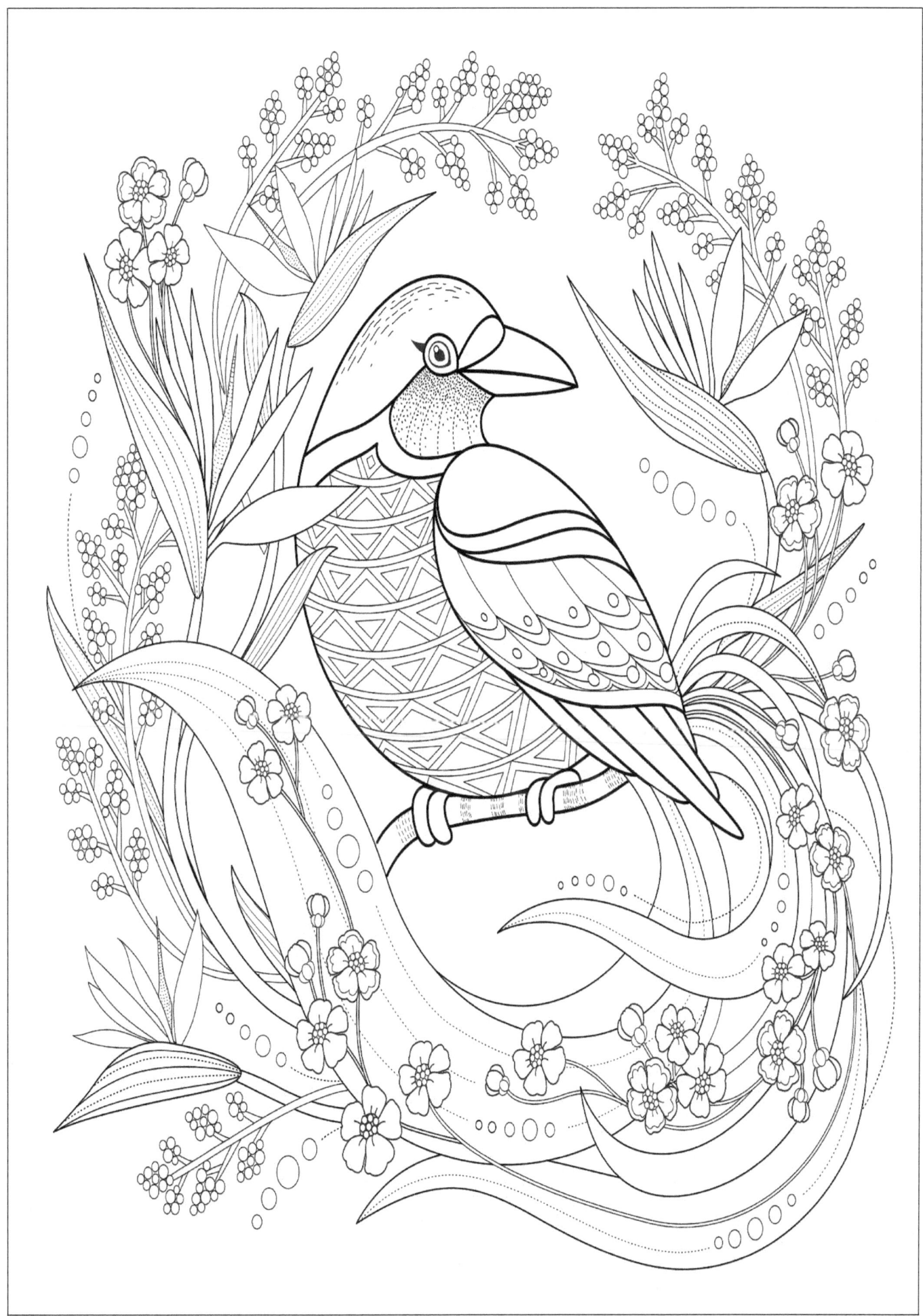

Level 2

Born to fly

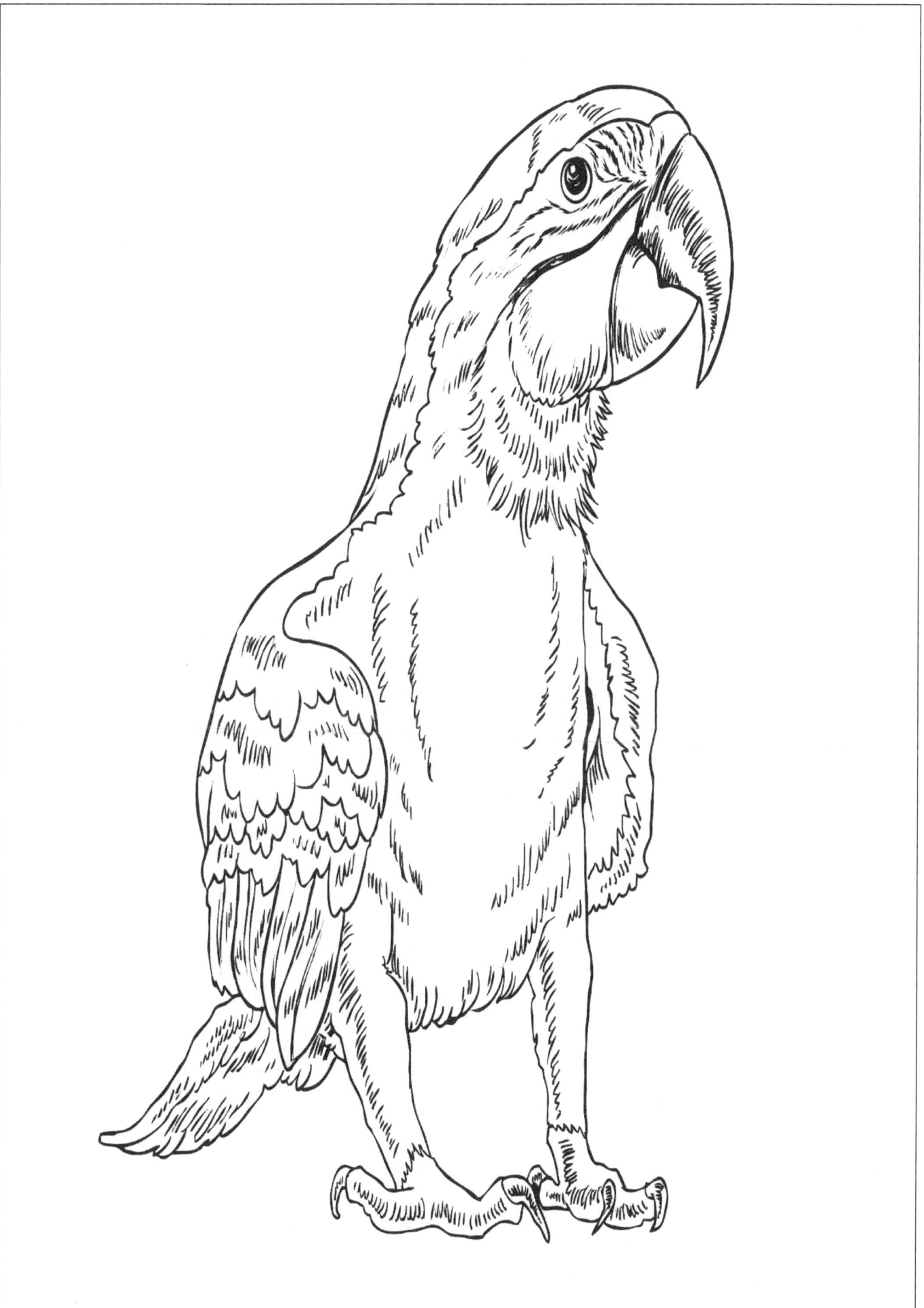

Level 2

Life is better with friends.

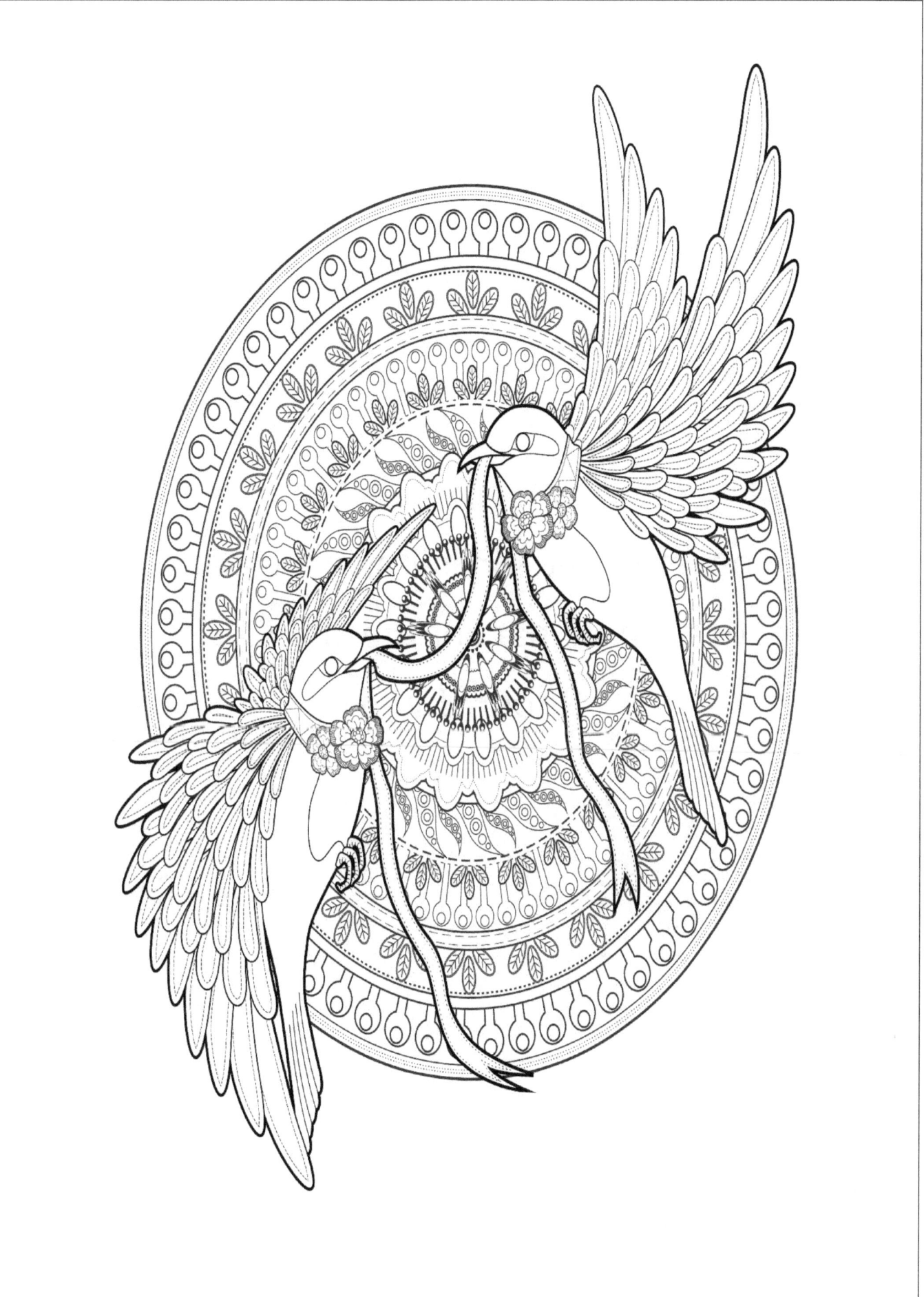

Level 2

In order to see birds it is necessary
to become part of the silence.
- Robert Lynd

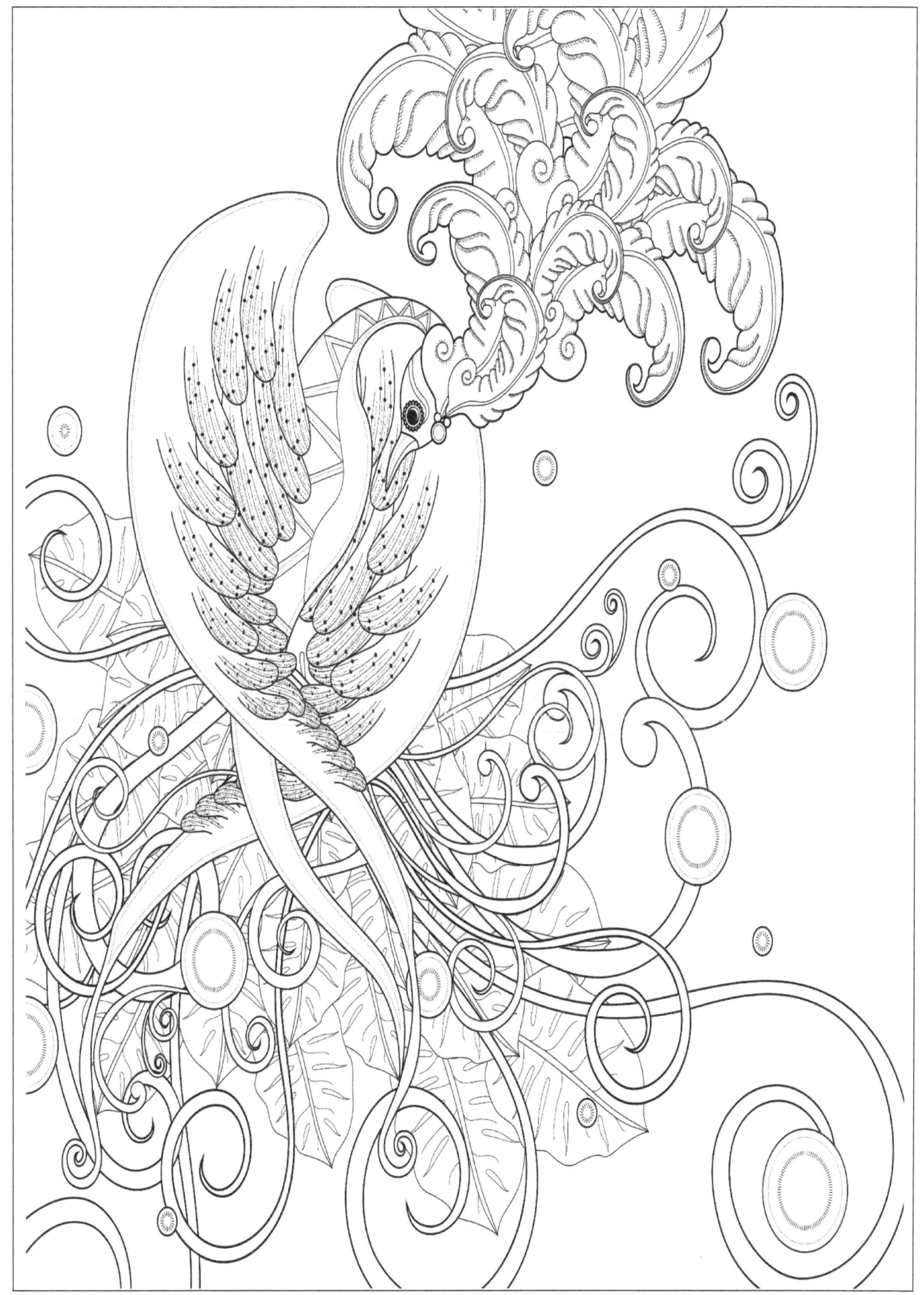

Level 3

One day you're a peacock.

The next day you're a feather duster.

- Author Unknown.

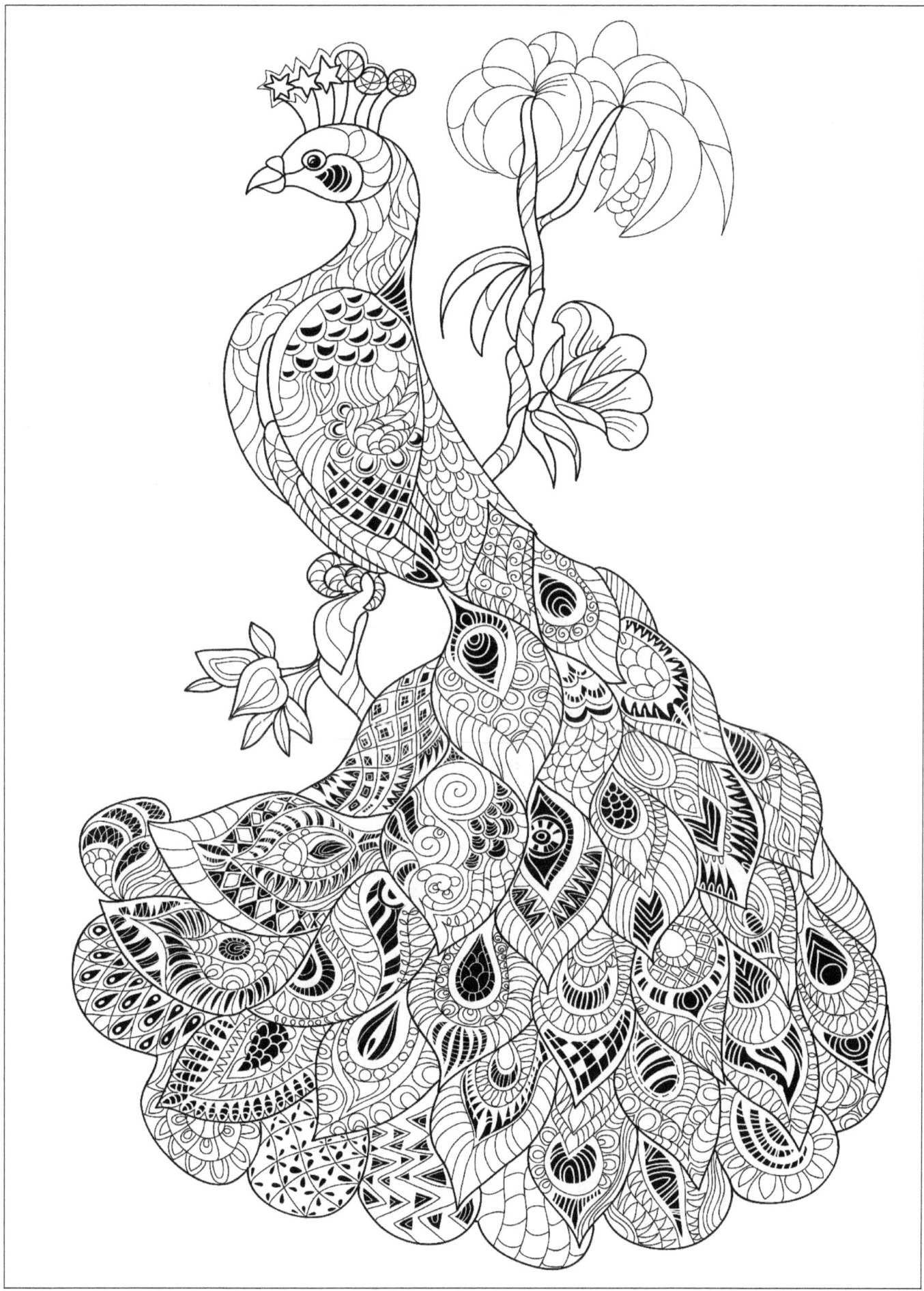

Level 2

For to have faith,

is to have wings.

- Peter Pan

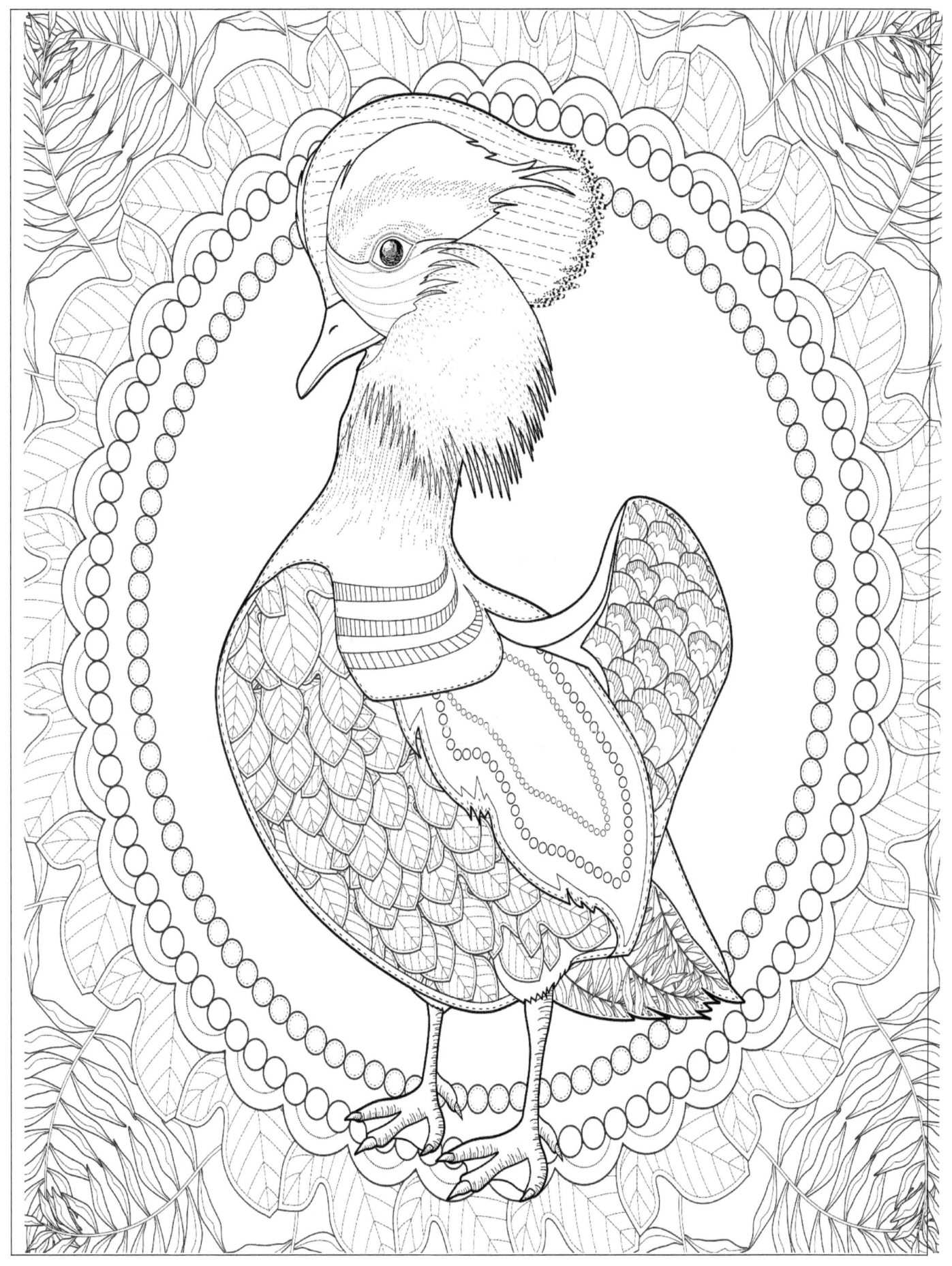

Level 2

I'm not afraid of flying.

I'm afraid of not flying.

- Author Unknown.

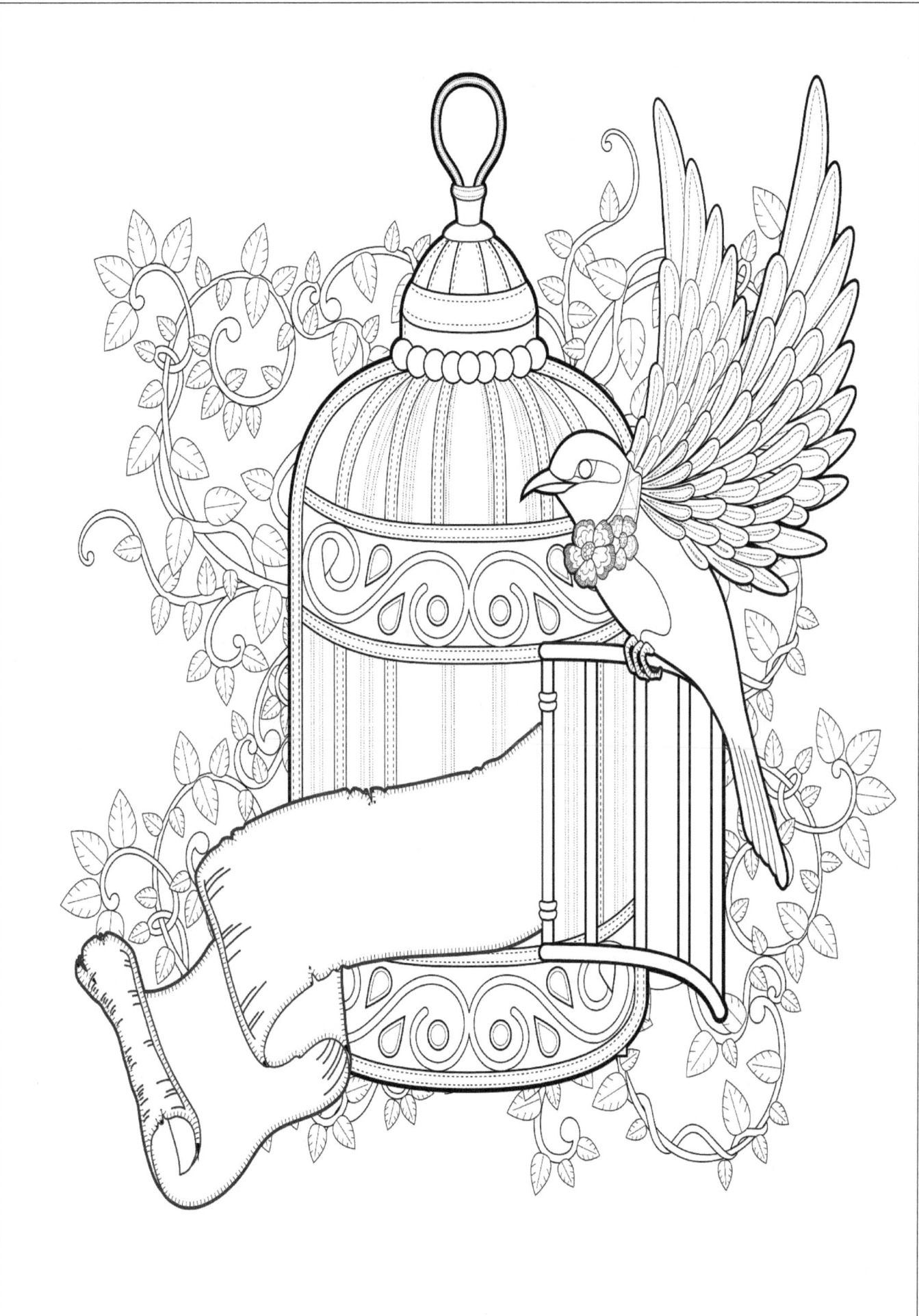

Level 3

Hold fast to dreams for if dreams die,
life is a broken-winged bird that cannot fly.
- Langston Hughes

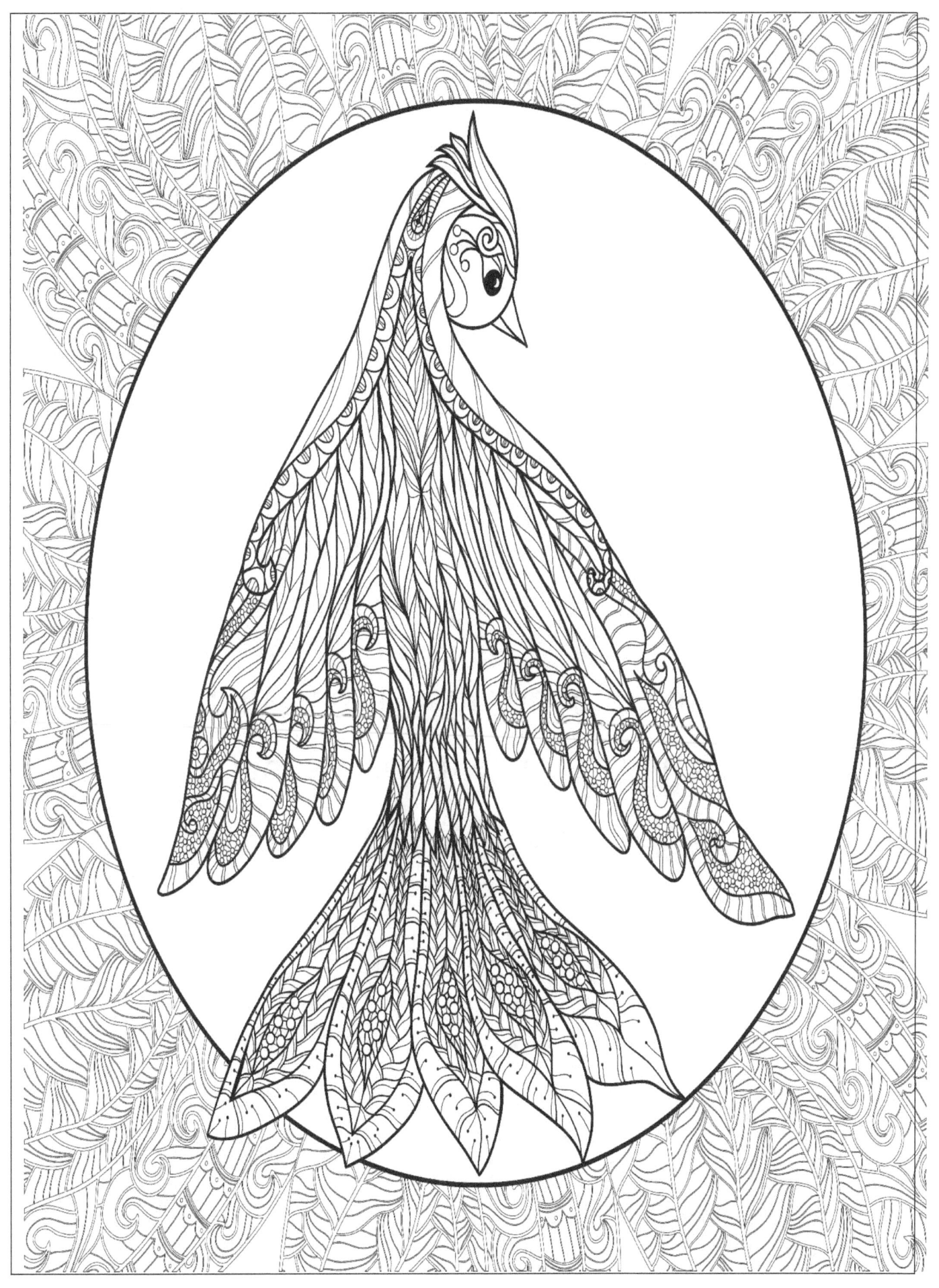

Level 3

A bird doesn't sing because it has an answer,

it sings because it has a song.

-Lou Holtz

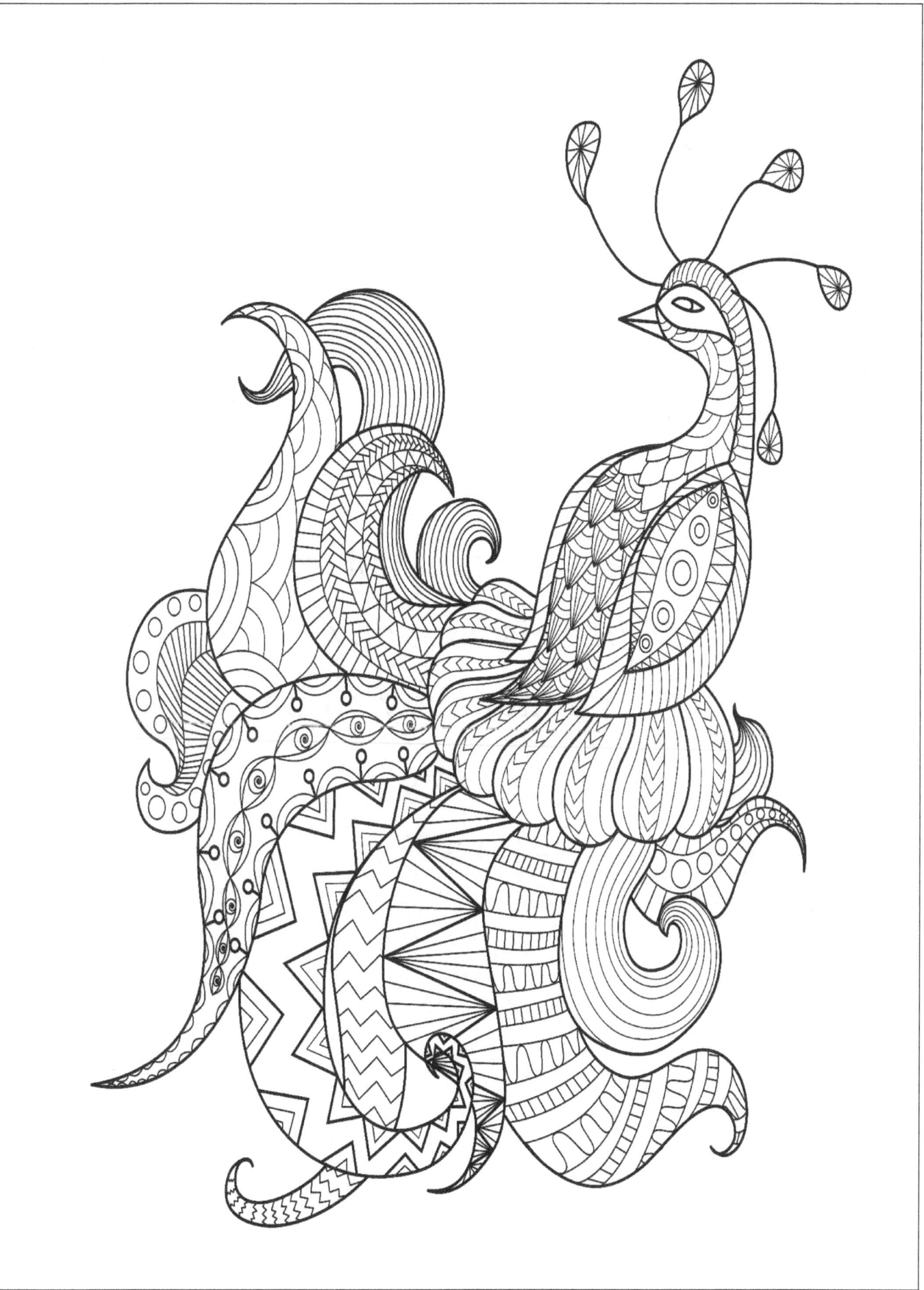

Level 2

You're off to great places!

Today is your day!

Your mountain is waiting!

So get on your way!

- Dr Seuss

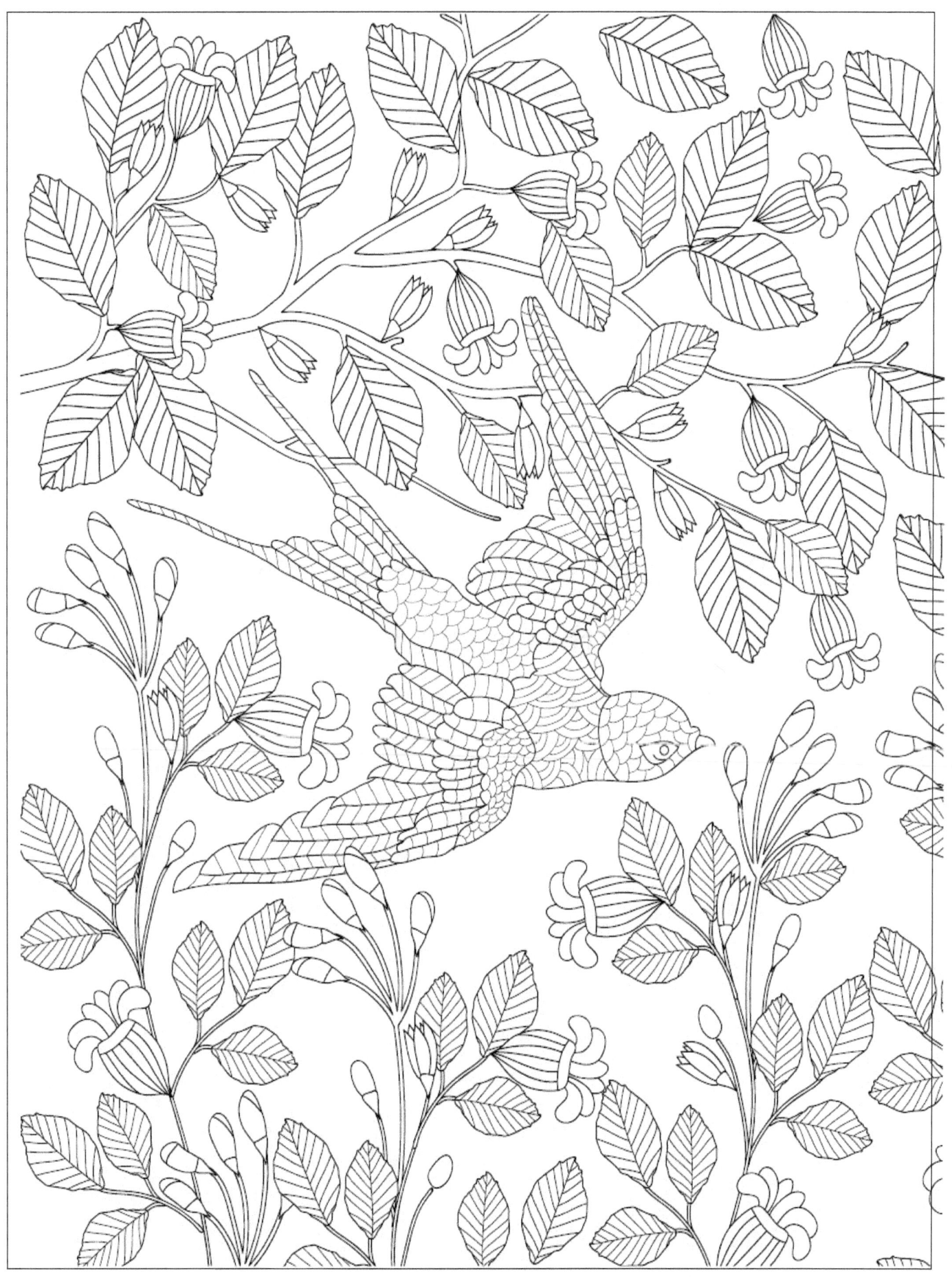

Level 3

Sing as if no one can hear you.

- Author unknown.

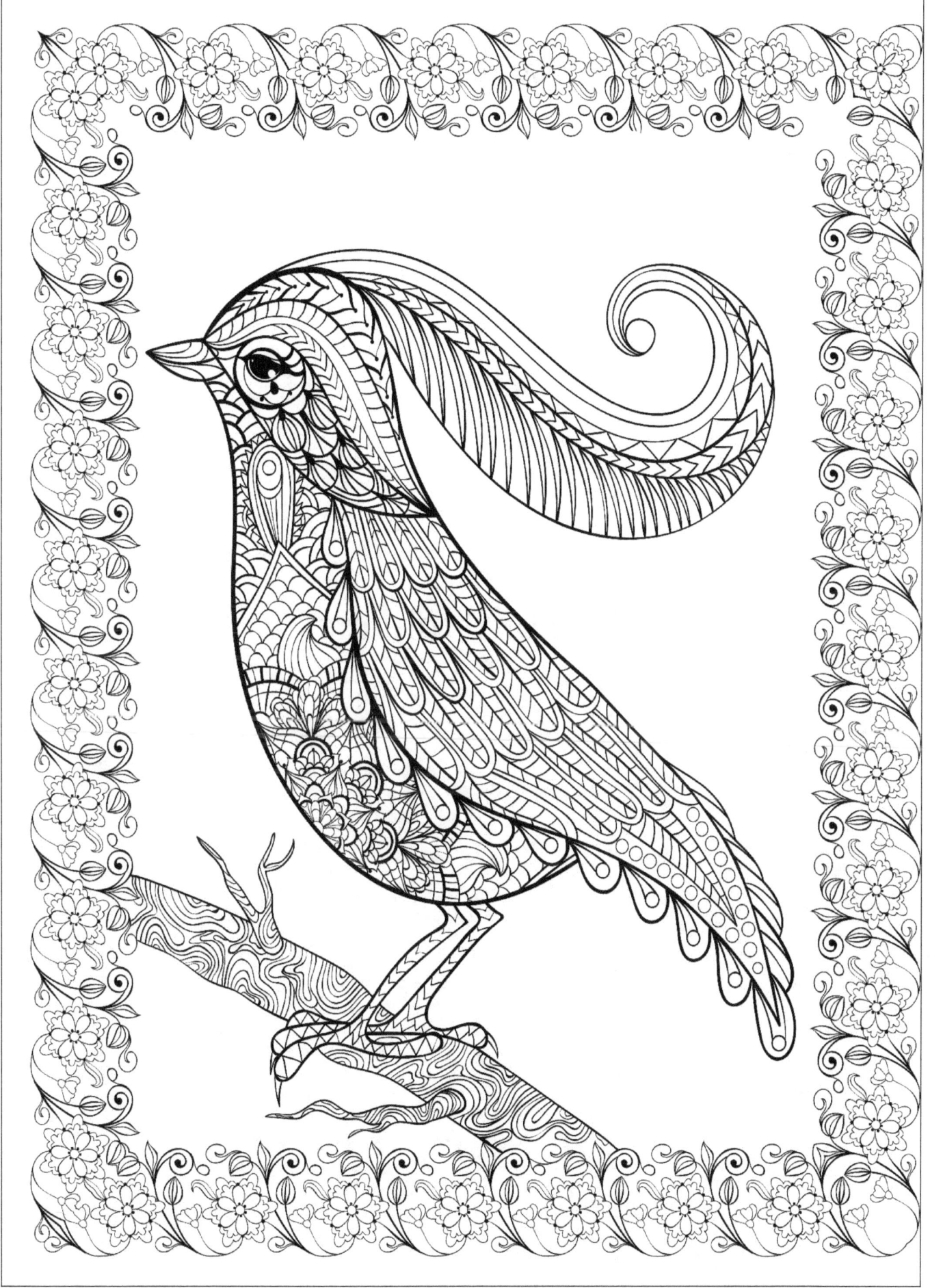

Level 1

.

A little bird told me.

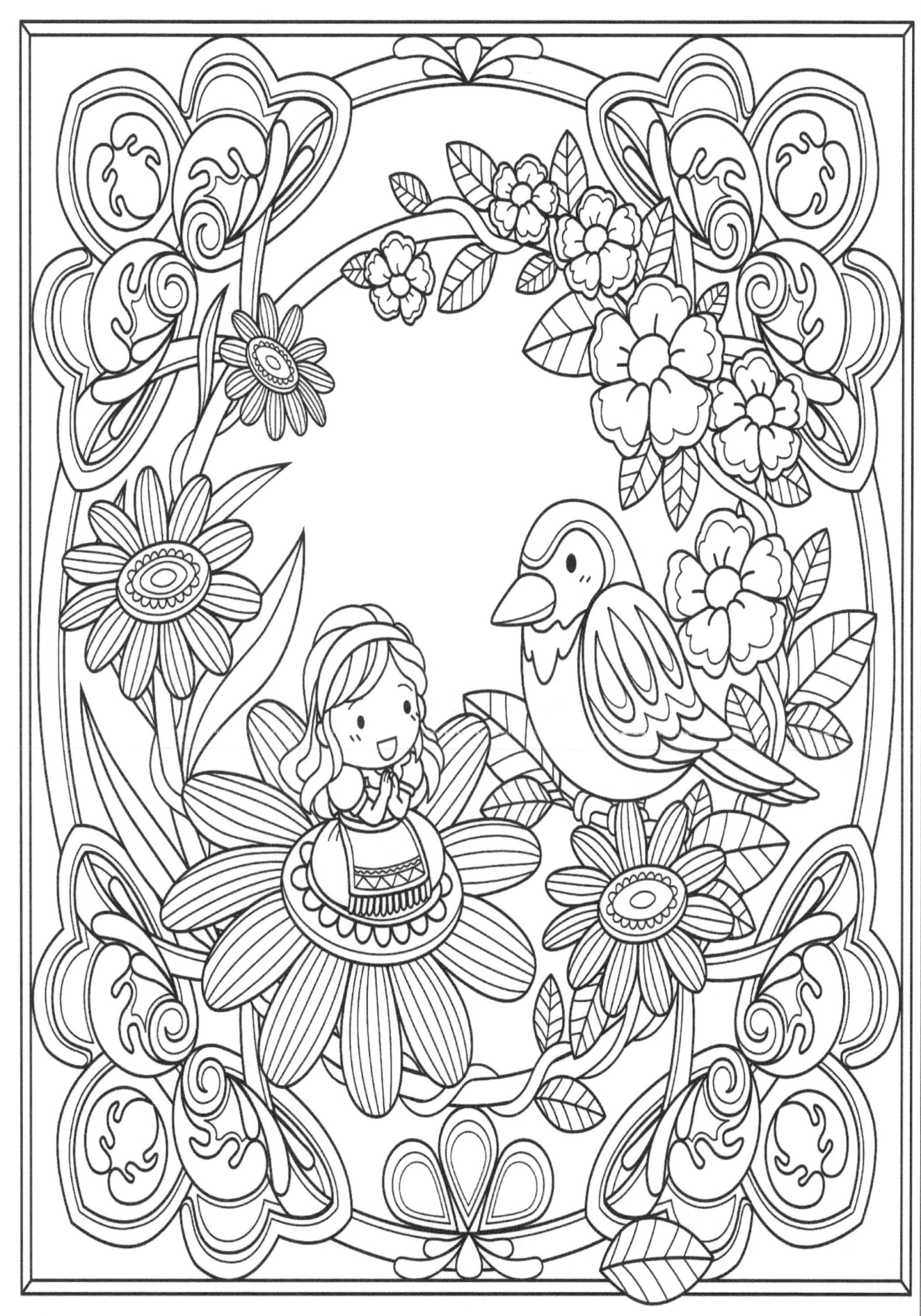

Level 2

Dare to fly.

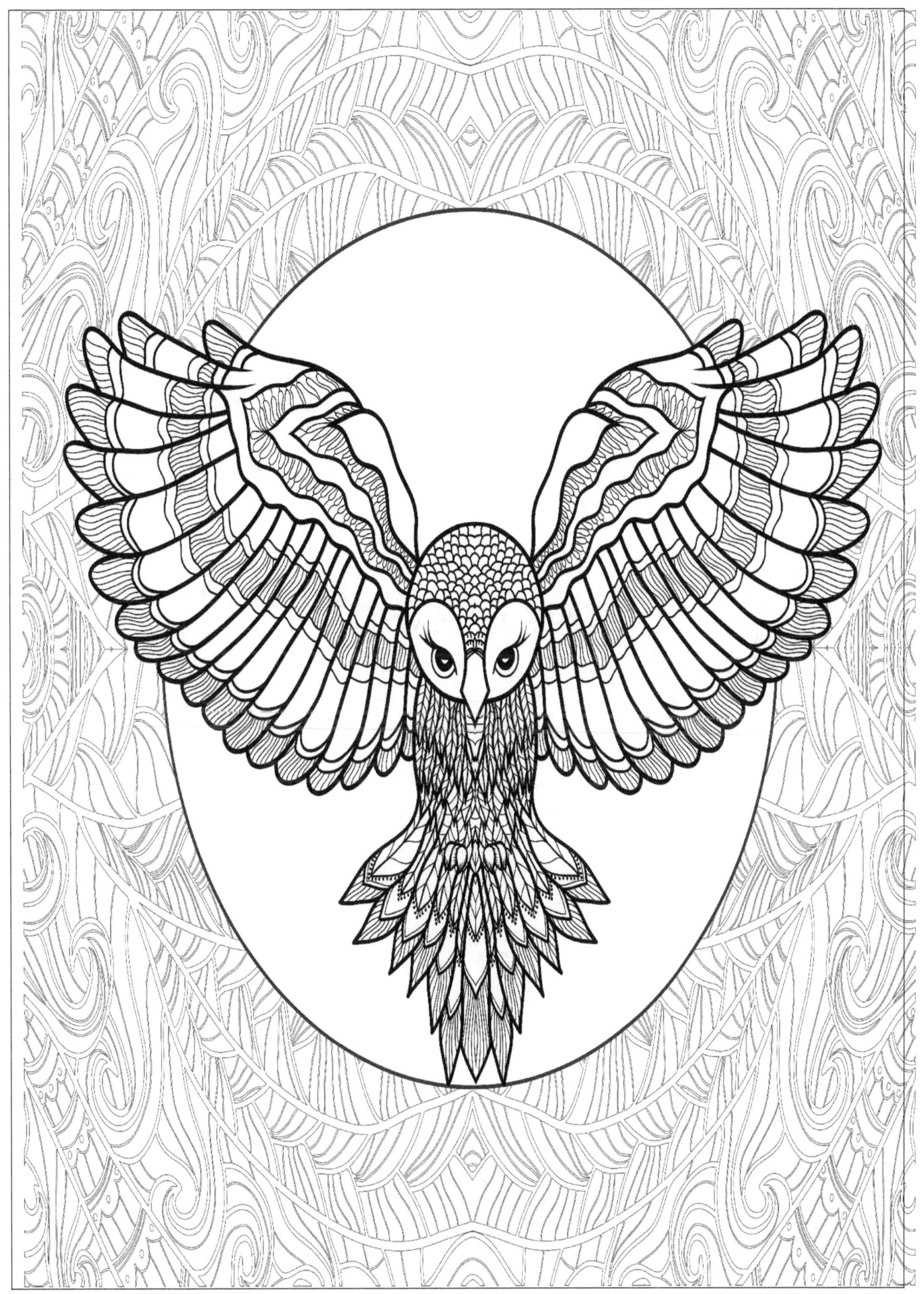

Level 1

Free as a bird.

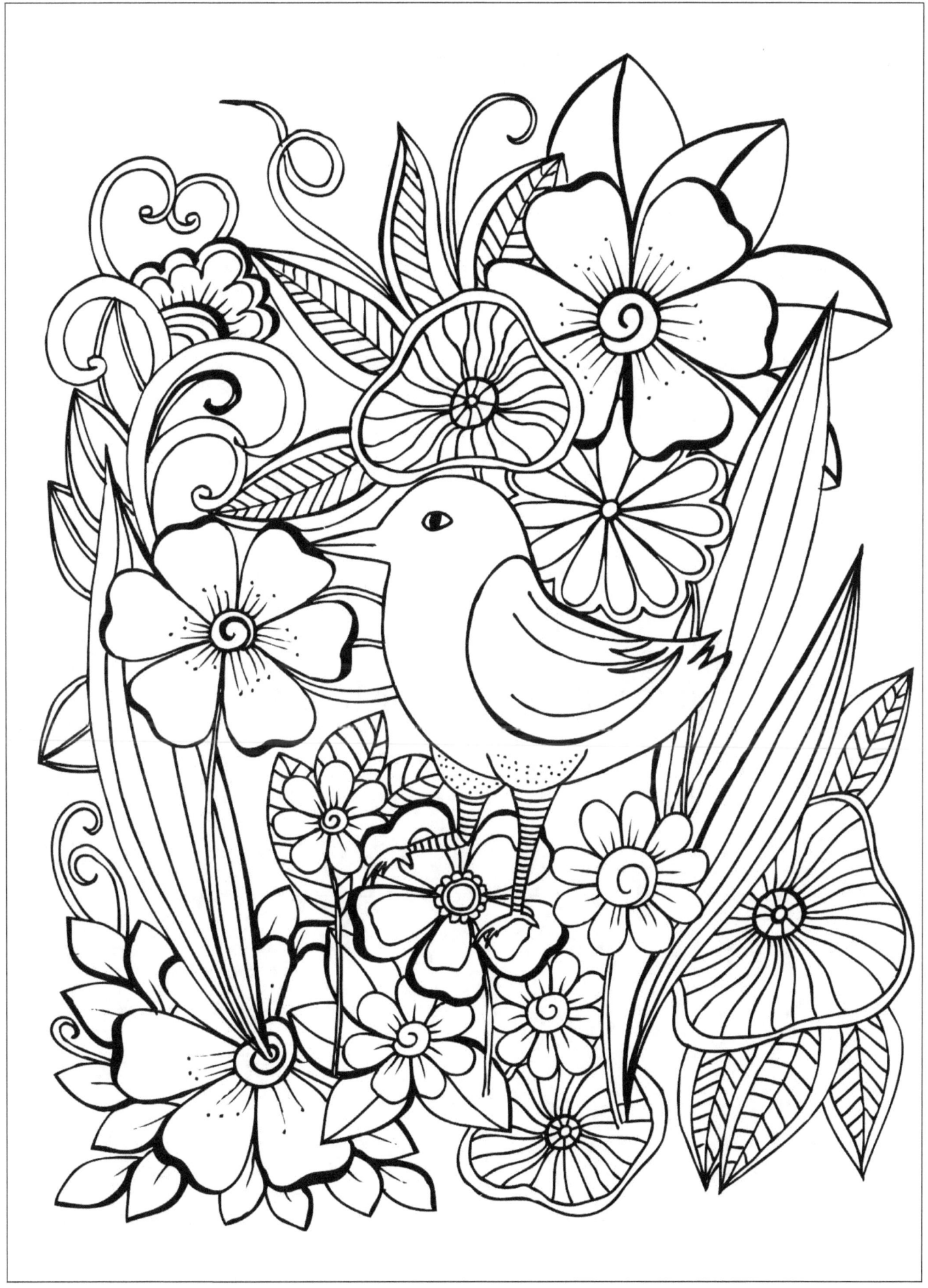

Level 2

Love with owl your heart.

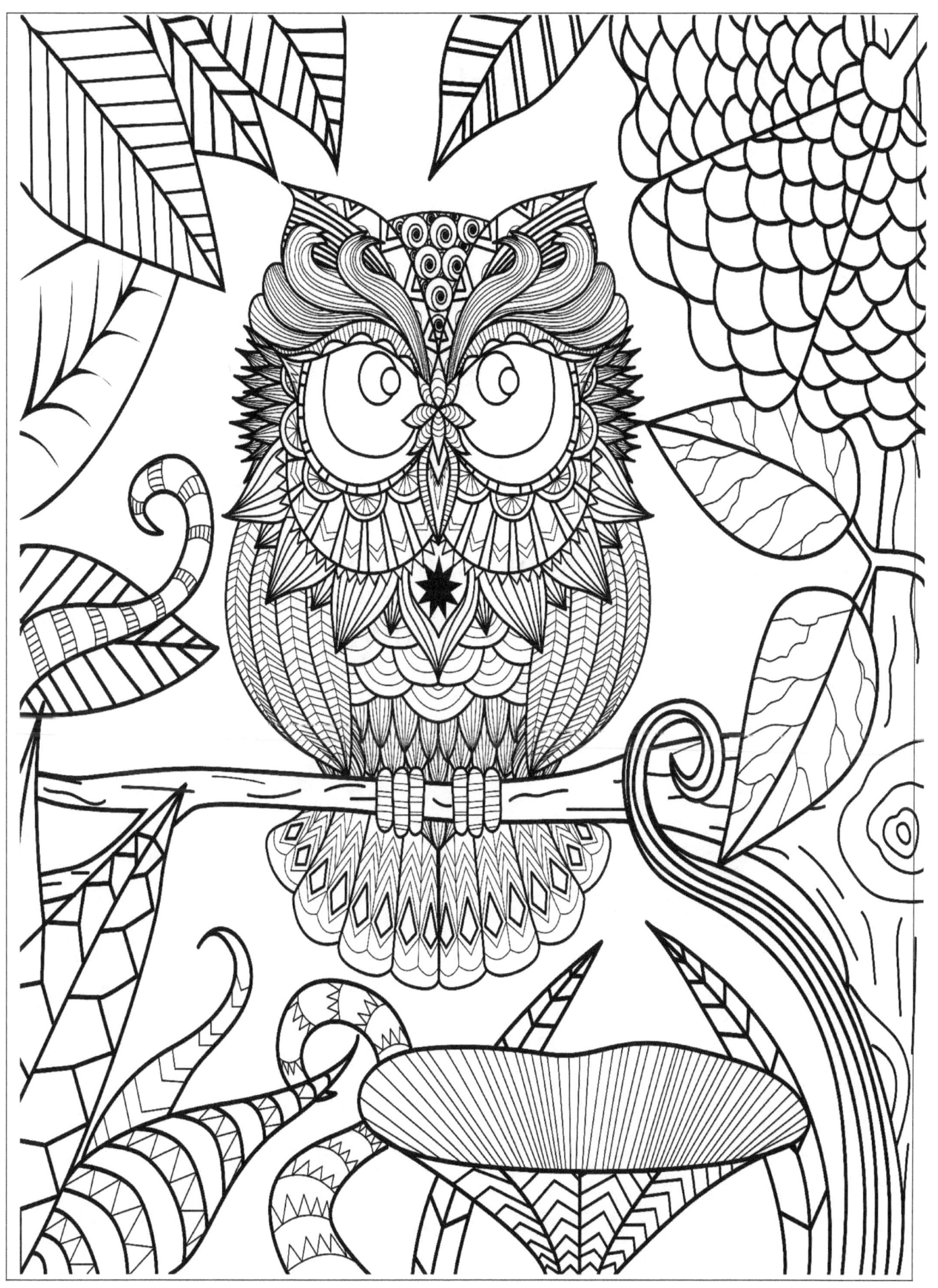

Level 2

The wisdom you seek is already within you.

Author Unknown.

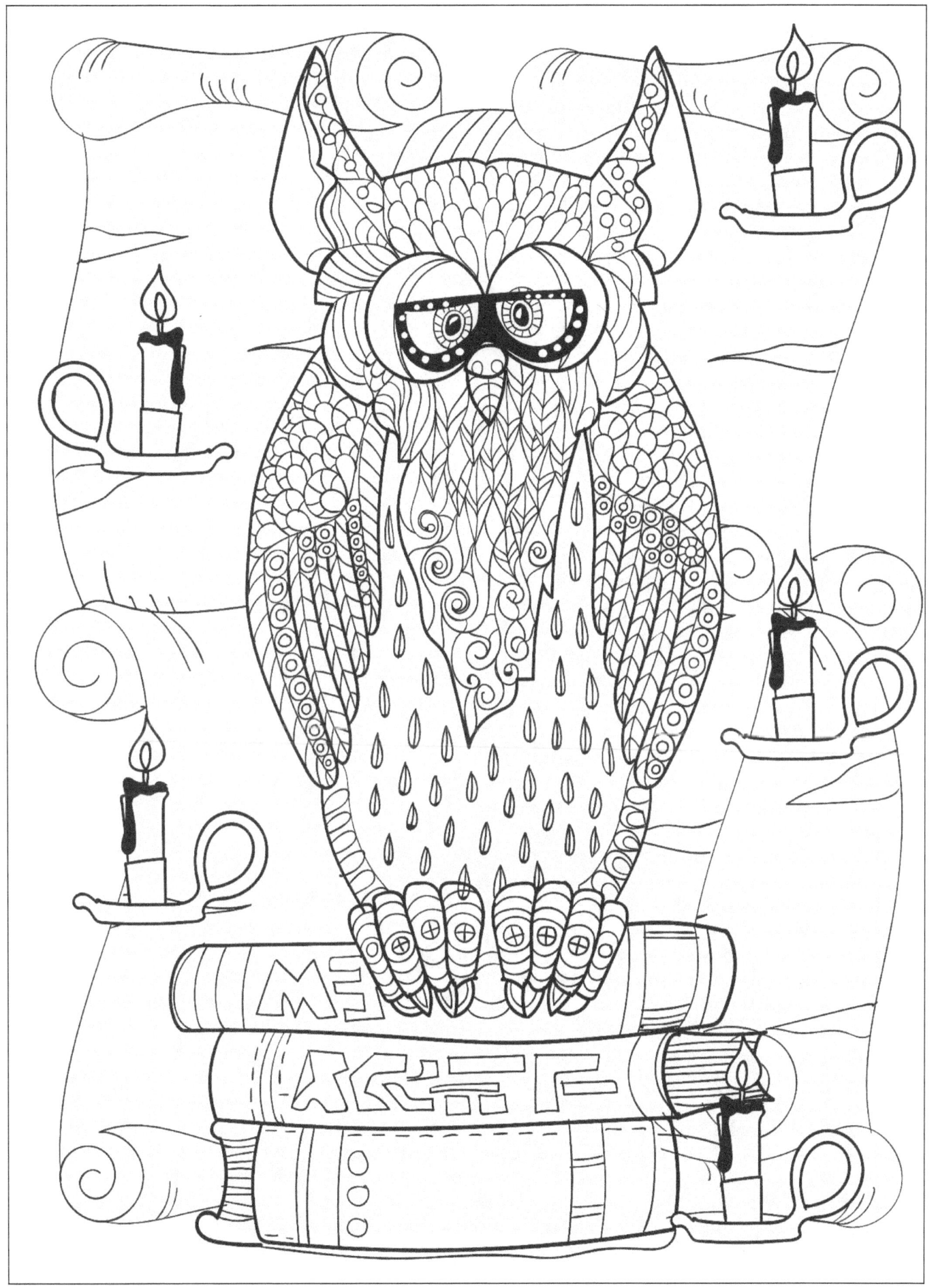

www.ingramcontent.com/pod-product-compliance
Lightning Source LLC
Chambersburg PA
CBHW080642180526
45168CB00008B/3277